CAPITALISM AND THE 'EVIL EMPIRE'

Reducing Superpower Conflict
Through
American Economic Reform

CAPITALISM AND THE 'EVIL EMPIRE'

Reducing Superpower Conflict Through American Economic Reform

Edited by

Kenneth B. Taylor

New Horizons Press
New York, New York

Copyright ©1988 by New Horizons Press

New Horizons Press is an imprint of the Council on International and Public Affairs, Inc., 777 United Nations Plaza, New York, New York 10017 (212/972-9877)

Library of Congress Cataloging-in-Publication Data

Capitalism and the 'evil empire' : reducing superpower conflict through American economic reform / edited by Kenneth B. Taylor .
    p.   cm.
  Bibliography: p.
  ISBN 0-945257-01-5
  1. Capitalism. 2. United States—Economic policy—1981- .
3. United States—Relations—Soviet Union.   4. Soviet Union—
Relations—United States.   I. Taylor, Kenneth B., 1950-   .
HB501.C24243 1988
338.973—dc19   88-25315

Typeset and printed in the United States of America

CONTENTS

ACKNOWLEDGEMENTS

This volume, which grew out of the 1984-85 Stuart M. Speiser Essay Contest on Expanded Capital Ownership, is the product of many hands. The essayists, of course, merit pride of place because there would have been no book, quite literally, without them. That is equally true of Professor Kenneth Taylor of the Department of Economics at Villanova University, who undertook the arduous task of achieving some measure of coherence out of a rich but diverse and inchoate mass of raw material extracted from some 300 essays submitted in the contest.

Stuart M. Speiser also played a key role by writing the book that inspired the contest *(How to End the Nuclear Nightmare)*, donating the prize money and contributing an epilogue to the book. The Trustees of the Council on International and Public Affairs serving on the Judging Panel of the Essay Contest, which was administered by the Council, likewise played an important supporting role.

Copy editing and production supervision was undertaken by Cynthia T. Morehouse, Director of Editorial Services for the Council. Peggy Hurley undertook composition of the book in record time.

Because of the pressures of time in getting the manuscript to press, some editorial changes could not be cleared with Professor Taylor who was on an overseas lecturing assignment for the 1987-88 academic year. While every effort has been made to preserve the general thrust of his skillful editing, the editorial staff of the Council takes final responsibility for the published version of the book.

I.

THE STUART M. SPEISER ESSAY CONTEST

How can we, without adopting socialism or giving up our treasured freedoms, modify American capitalism to make it more equitable and reduce the level of ideological conflict with the Soviet Union so as to make possible an end to the nuclear nightmare?

So began the announcement distributed by the Council on International and Public Affairs in 1984 on the occasion of the first Speiser Essay Contest. Stuart Speiser had addressed this question in his book, *How to End the Nuclear Nightmare*, and outlined a new social program which, if instituted, was claimed to have the potential to reduce hostilities between the superpowers as well as promote economic democracy for future generations of Americans. SuperStock was what he called his proposed social program in this book, but in subsequent work renamed it the Kitty Hawk model of a Universal Share Ownership Plan (USOP).[1]

Before going any further let us reflect on the theme of this competition. The question above makes several implicit assumptions which channeled the creative efforts of those who sought to answer it. First, it assumes that the ideological conflict is central to relations between the US and the Soviet Union. Second, American economic reform directed at ameliorating the ideological gulf between the superpowers is assumed to lead causally to a reduction in international tensions between the two. Finally, as tension diminishes, it is implied that the superpowers will be motivated to act more peacefully in the world and to "build-down" their respective nuclear stockpiles. The reader may disagree with the chain of logic represented by these primary assumptions, as many essayists did, yet the working hypothesis which they form created the stage for an enlightening dialogue.

One other fundamental assumption of the question is that in order to create lasting peace our socioeconomic system must change. True peace will not come without uniform societal justice. Without comprehensive justice within a nation, and between nations, promotion of peace will not include the total commitment required. All attempts at world governance and diplomatic negotiation in the context of even partially unjust nations will serve only to lengthen the nuclear fuse. Although America has attained a high degree of sociopolitical justice, the collective opinion of the essayists was that economic justice is seriously lacking. The retarded development of the institutions of economic justice form the foundation upon which the nuclear confrontation between the Soviets and Americans is supported.

There is no intention here to put more responsibility for the superpowers' problems on America. If anything, the Soviet institutions of justice are much more seriously underdeveloped. Of the two nations, as Speiser points out in his book, only the American system has within it the tradition and flexibility to respond. Speiser would argue that given the ultimate dimensions of the problems the superpowers face, America has a moral responsibility to take all actions consistent with its Constitution that will enhance the prospects for world peace.

In working on this volume the editor researched the existing capitalist literature on creating world peace as well as the literature on suggested economic reforms for the US. It is of interest to also note in this introduction that, with the exception of the work of Speiser, no other work relates capitalist economic reform to the promotion of world peace. Typical of the world peace literature were the results of *The Christian Science Monitor's* "Peace 2010" contest. A synopsis of the 1,300 essays submitted to this contest can be found in the book, *How Peace Came to the World.*[2] With a few exceptions to be soon noted, the vast majority of writers developed scenarios where external world events trigger internal national change from which a more peaceful world emerges. In very few scenarios did conscious, before-the-fact action play any role in the emergence of world peace.

In one typical essay a newly inaugurated American president unilaterally shifts a large percentage of the US military budget to domestic programs; the Soviets react to this window of opportunity by making a similar budgetary move and a series of events are set in motion to effectively reduce the arms race. Another small group of authors argued that a fundamental change in consciousness is under way in the world. Weaving together the "pardigm shift" of Daniel Bell, the "changing image of man" of Willis Harman, and Kenneth Boulding's notion of a "new region of time," several writers indicated that it was only a matter of time before a new world order centered on peace and justice would emerge.

The flaw in the first type of "internal change" argument is that the confrontation between the superpowers is not so deeply rooted that the nuclear house of cards will collapse if only we pull out the right card. It was indicated earlier that the Speiser Essay Contest operated under the implicit assumption that diplomacy and efforts at world governance only treat the symptoms, leaving the disease untouched. In other words, our problems have deep roots. A fundamental error in the second set of "internal change" scenarios presented in the "Peace 2010" contest is that the change in consciousness now occurring in the world is uniform. It is not, and to believe so is naive. The Soviet Union, among many others, is an Orwellian state lacking freedom of speech, information and ideas. A universal change in consciousness can take place only in an environment where thoughts and facts can move freely. Given the non-uniformity of the present change in consciousness, it may be centuries before that change becomes global. Another premise of the Speiser Essay Contest is that we do not have the luxury of waiting for peace or justice to arise naturally.

Before leaving our discussion of the "Peace 2010" contest behind, it is of interest to note that the editors reported ". . . that a majority of entrants felt any realistic plan for peace in the next quarter century would have to deal with the Soviet-American rivalry first."[3] This fact Stuart Speiser realizes and is the reason he focused the competition's question on the superpowers.

The literature on proposals to reform capitalism is centered on enhancing American living standards, macroeconomic stability and/or economic justice. A current example of a proposal to improve the US standard of living is to institutionalize an industrial policy. As Lester Thurow has put it: "They [industrial policies] outline the basic strategy the nation intends to follow in maximizing economic growth and meeting foreign competition."[4] Martin Weitzman's well-developed "share economy" concept is concerned with the triple problems of persistent unemployment, inflation and slow economic growth.[5] His solution is to correct an underlying structural flaw in the nature of labor renumeration and suggests an alternative payment system where wages are tied to some appropriate index of a firm's performance. This new payment system he outlines would restore downward flexible wage rates and consequently boost employment, lower inflation, create higher income for labor in general and potentially reduce the incidence of poverty. In *The Next American Frontier* Robert Reich suggests a strategy for renewing America's social and economic institutions. In part he suggests an educational voucher system, allowing the unemployed to get on-the-job instruction in industries with a future, and tax reform geared toward making corporations more responsible in their investing and to the workers they lay off. Reich argues that if his proposals are enacted, they will bring economic growth and lower unemployment.[6]

There already are many good ideas in circulation on constructive reform of the American economic system, of which only a few have been mentioned here. None of the popular capitalist economic reform literature that was reviewed, however, addressed the issue of the increasingly unequal distribution of income and wealth which capitalism tends to engender. No literature could be found, outside the Marxist/socialist camp, which links the issues of world peace, ideology and national economic reform. Herein lies the uniqueness of the Speiser Essay Competition, for it asked each entrant to consider the interrelationship between these three issues outside of the Marxian rhetoric. Whether or not these three issues are truely linked was the ultimate question to be addressed by the essayists.

Much of what follows may appear abstract, yet underlying it all is the awesome reality that mankind has the power to destroy life on earth. This power is spreading from nation state to nation state with no known means of control. Any discussion of the path to the future cannot escape the guise of abstraction since tomorrow has yet to come. Something shared by all who wrote for this competition (approximately 300) was a deep realization that the world is accelerating into the future on a path which is becoming increasingly narrow. On one side lies the cliff of nuclear Armegeddon, on the other the cliff of injustice, suffering and dispair. Larry Marshall states in his essay, "Synergistic Solutions: A Tapestry of Great Power": ". . . I say, 'Why not dream? The alternative is catastrophe! . . . It is only the dreamers who can save us.'"[7] It may very well be time for us to begin to listen to the dreamers.

The Speiser Proposal

SuperStock represents an institution of "universal" capitalism, whereby all Americans can become true capitalists through the ownership of corporate stock. In 1977 the Brookings Institution held an all-day seminar which was attended by economists, financial experts and government officials. From a technical perspective, none of the individuals who attended this seminar could find serious flaws in the design of Speiser's model of a USOP.

In Speiser's opinion the majority of America's domestic and international problems originate from the inequitable distribution of capital ownership and income. Citing the studies by Frank Levy and Richard Michel, as well as economists at the Urban Institute, he observes that the gap between the rich and poor continues to widen. From this he concludes that "trickledown" economics is failing despite the existence of the progressive income tax structure and the social welfare apparatus. Speiser argues that if this trend continues it will be only a matter of time before American voters choose some form of pension fund socialism. This, he fears, would cause the American economic engine to grind to a halt with a gradual disintegration of the basic civil liberties we enjoy.

Speiser argues that it is possible to use capitalism to save capitalism—to create an institution which is built upon the strength of capitalism, the ability of physical capital to pay for itself and which will allow all US citizens to participate in capitalism as capitalists. He goes on to query:

> But consider: if capitalism could be made universal, if we could in one generation equalize the wealth of the nation as SuperStock is designed to do, what threat would Marxism pose to the United States? If the system worked for everyone, why would voters seek to alter it? If everyone becomes an owner, there would be nobody left to exploit; thus, capitalism and Marxism would no longer be divided over the central issue of class struggle to overcome exploitation.[8]

From these thoughts he makes the further deduction that elimination of the source of ideological contention between the US and the USSR would constitute a major step in the direction of creating the atmosphere of mutual trust upon which the goals of nuclear disarmament and peace between the two can be attained. Finally, he concludes that elimination of the basis of class warfare will halt worldwide Marxist revolution paving the way for global peace and democracy.

To set up a USOP will require congressional legislation—a "USOP Act." While the basic outline of Speiser's SuperStock model is simple, the reader will realize the details to be much more complicated. Some of those details have been addressed in this volume, others have been addressed in a second contest also sponsored by Stuart Speiser and administered by the Council on International and Public Affairs in 1986.

The Council plans to publish some of the leading essays in the near future.

According to Speiser's plan, the legislation institutionalizing the program will mandate that the 2,000 largest American corporations participate. Once a firm is designated to participate, it will no longer finance its capital expansion plans through a combination of common stock, preferred stock, debt and retained earnings. When a firm needs money for capital expansion, it will obtain it through the USOP apparatus by issuing a new form of stock which we will refer to here as USOP shares. The USOP is obligated to accept the newly issued USOP shares and to provide the participating firm with an equal dollar amount of checkable deposits. To finance any new USOP stock issue, the USOP will issue debt instruments in the private capital markets. Using capital outlay figures in the recent past, Speiser argues that business requires approximately $300 billion each year to finance new capital. In roughly 20 years the central USOP account will amass $5 trillion worth of USOP shares.

To liquidate the debt which was floated to finance USOP shares, all corporate earnings will be required to be paid out as dividends to the USOP. The only exception allowed would be a small pool of retained earnings for daily operations and unforeseen contingencies. All USOP shares will be held in escrow until the dividends flowing in pay off the debt initially incurred. At this point, the paid-off USOP shares will be owned free and clear by the American citizens to whom they have been distributed.

Speiser's proposal here is to distribute USOP shares to Americans who presently are not capitalists and do not enjoy the income generating potential of capital ownership. To prevent any gross inequities, Speiser proposes that the USOP distribute risk by creating a mutual fund or unit trust. Recipients would then receive a portfolio of mutual fund shares from the USOP. Once in the citizens' hands, all future dividends from the paid-off USOP shares will be paid directly to them. Speiser suggests that the first recipients might all be households with a current net worth below $100,000. As an alternative, he suggests that a point system for eligibility be established. In any case, if the $5 trillion figure were to be divided among the present 50 million non-capitalist households, each would eventually hold a USOP portfolio worth $100,000. Assuming a 20 per cent return on invested capital, this would provide each of these households with about $20,000 per year in dividend income.

Speiser hopes that the USOP would, over time, replace both our Social Security and welfare programs. If his figures are correct, the necessary income would definitely be there to do so. The editor has left out of this discussion many aspects of the plan which Speiser does present in his book. Some of these aspects will be gleaned from the papers which follow; all can be found in his book. In essence, this is the plan which the participants of the Brookings' seminar studied and the one the Joint Economic Committee of Congress found promising in 1976.

Who Will Lose?

Speiser states that the SuperStock plan would create a more equitable distribution of income and would do so without affecting the existing distribution of ownership or income. Since SuperStock is based on ownership of future capital, no confiscation of wealth or reshuffling of present income is necessary. This statement is true up until the first USOP shares are issued. At that point, intertemporal and intergenerational subtleties emerge which clearly indicate that the existing capitalists have much to lose.

One of the entrants in the essay contest, Jane Dillion, put it most succinctly in her essay, "Selling SuperStock":

> It seems to me that there will only be one group of people who will clearly lose something. That doesn't sound like much of a problem, but unfortunately it is the richest, most powerful group in the country: the original stockholders who will be expecting a yearly increase of their shareholdings, and under SuperStock will not get it. Super-Stockholders will be buying these shares instead, and the original stockholders will be left only with their original stocks.

> Speiser deals with this issue by convincing us that the "pie" will be larger and that the original stockholders will in fact own a lesser portion of a bigger pie and in the long run, this will work out fine. It is essential that Speiser and others are able to convince the original stockholders of this fact. Speiser must be prepared to deal with this issue effectively against the natural and expected complaints of the original stockholders, their lawyers, their congressmen and their businesses. It comes as no surprise that this 6 per cent of the population is the very 6 per cent that has a controlling influence over much of what happens in the US. SuperStock must truly be advantageous to the country, to business, to capitalism, for it to survive this very influential group's interest, and the people representing SuperStock must be prepared. Altruism will not be enough. SuperStock must be sold to the 6 per cent not on the basis of threats and fear, but on the basis of benefit to them; that they will not lose money, but stand to gain a stronger, more secure economy in which they own a share.[9]

If USOP legislation is promoted as a key to nuclear disarmament and peace, another powerful constituency would also stand to lose. In another essay in the contest, "Devolution: A Path to Stable Peace," Donald Clark argues that America needs a comprehensive restructuring which will redistribute power from the federal level to the local level. In discussing the process of redistributing decision-making power, he makes an interesting observation which is also relevant to a USOP:

> Any hope of negotiating our way through this minefield to a new balance between local and federal power is severely compromised by the presence of our national mascot, the military dinosaur. The President, with majority backing, perpetuates the myth about America's global mission and the mortal threat inherent in the Soviet Union's pretensions to an equal global status. His advocacy of military strength has negated every effort to decrease government size, and is corrupting the free enterprise foundations of business with military contracts. The most obvious face of the nuclear nightmare is the threat of mass destruction; but there is another face: a society in which every effort to adapt to the demands of a new generation and the challenges of international trade is blocked by a huge, inflexible military-political-industrial complex supporting a thoroughly militarized economy.[10]

Disarmament and peace would mean lost jobs and lost business for the military establishment and the myriad industries which sell billions of dollars of goods annually to the military. There is no arguing that these constituencies are plugged into the political process and since they would lose, they undoubtedly would resist.

Introduction to the Essays and Their Authors

This volume is organized around six essays submitted to the Speiser Essay Contest, including the prize-winning essay. These are introduced or followed by commentary by the editor, which has been drawn from ideas presented by a number of other essayists participating in the contest. In some instances significant excerpts from these essays, labeled "Contributions" in the text, have been included in the editor's commentaries in order to convey something of the richness and diversity of submissions to the contest.

Ideologically, the entrants ranged from Marxist to Libertarian. Some focused on fine-tuning the USOP concept; others made dramatically different proposals. Socialized land rent, monetary reform, effective world government, worker-self-management are but a sampling of the proposals set forth. Several essays centered on the ideological question and the US-Soviet world power struggle; others ignored these issues completely. Few essays gave equal attention to the questions of peace, economic reform and the role of ideology. In selecting the papers to be included in their entirety, the editor looked for original perspectives and realistic proposals in the context of the contest question. All six authors seem to accept the premise that the distribution of income and wealth is becoming more unequal over time. What is interesting is that given existing institutions, increased inequality was forecast for *any* future economic growth scenario. Speiser, and many of the essayists, viewed economic growth in the future to continue on the historical, exponential trend line fed by the revolution in high technology. Even this "high growth" view was seen as generating greater income inequality.

In Speiser's book he presents the primary means by which an individual becomes wealthy. He argues that 95 per cent of new capital expenditures are financed through debt and internal funds—only 5 per cent is financed through issuance of new stock. When an investment is successful, those who reap the profits are not the debt holders—their return is fixed—but rather the common shareholders. This mechanism of financial leverage magnifies returns many-fold and remains the exclusive province of the already rich—the 6 per cent of Americans who are currently capitalists. One might argue that a firm's employees would benefit through higher wages. The problem is that the current revolution in technology has the potential to displace workers to an extent and at a rate unprecedented in the history of the industrial revolution. Expanding on this, Speiser notes:

> ... The robot—the steel collar worker—can work twenty-four hours a day, seven days a week, without making a mistake or getting bored. In 1983, American manufacturers could rent assembly-line robots at a total cost of six dollars an hour—robots that could do the work of humans who are paid three or four times as much for doing the job less efficiently. The Japanese are already using robots in large numbers, and we'll have to follow suit if we hope to remain competitive. Studies by the Congressional Budget Office and other groups estimate that automation and robots will eliminate three million manufacturing jobs by 1990 and another four million between 1990 and 2000. The age of robotics is nearly upon us, but we are still relying mainly on wages to make capitalism work, and our great thinkers seem to be unaware of a monumental question: Who will own the robots?[11]

Present statistics do not reveal a significant displacement of workers by high technology, yet it has the potential to do so. There is a long-run financial incentive for firms to substitute the new technologies for the old and the record of the recent past is in no way indicative of what will occur tomorrow.[12] If massive displacement does occur, many workers will be relegated to lower paying service sector employment while the owners of the means of production watch their wealth multiply.

Another contingent of essayists took the Kahn, Brown and Martel scenario of "gentle saturation."[13] In this view economic growth will continue but at an increasingly slower rate. This analysis is an outgrowth of the debate begun in the early 1970s by the Club of Rome concerning exponential growth of economic output, population and pollution. After years of research and refinement Kahn, Brown and Martel, all then working at the Hudson Institute, concluded that upcoming growth is more likely to follow a flattened S-shaped curve than to be either radically curtailed (systemic collapse) or exponential (the historical trend). With slower economic growth, other mechanisms in addition to those involving high technology come into play, worsening the income/wealth gap. These are discussed in greater depth elsewhere in this volume.

All essayists accept Speiser's conclusion that existing approaches to the nuclear arms issue prepare our society to be the kind of society which will use nuclear weapons, detract from economic growth in the long term and serve only to put off the day when nuclear weapons will be used. US intelligence surveys estimate that more than 30 nations will possess nuclear weapons by the year 2000. The Non-Proliferation Treaty is doomed to fail since the arms race between the superpowers undermines its integrity. As more and more nations acquire "the bomb," the probability of a nuclear exchange somewhere rises dramatically. To borrow a few words from an essayist in the "Peace 2010" contest:

> It is true that we have maintained stable nuclear deterrence for nearly forty years, but it is a mathematically certain proposition that deterrence cannot be stable in the long run. If it were stable, if the probability of nuclear weapons going off were zero, they would not deter anybody. The stability of deterrence in the short run necessitates its eventual breakdown . . . .[14]

Thus, the prospects for increasing inequality in the distribution of income and wealth as well as the long-term, non-viability of the politics of nuclear deterrence appeared to provide the basic motivation for the essayists in the Speiser Essay Contest. The role of ideology in all this was much less widely agreed upon. Some have dismissed it; others have reduced it in importance; still others have taken the creation of ideological compatibility as a working hypothesis and made astute suggestions toward attaining this goal.

The first essay in the book is by Jon Wisman, the winner of the contest. Professor Wisman is in the economics department of the American University in Washington, D.C. He has been a prolific writer and a recipient of the Helen Potter Award in Social Economics. His essay is quite critical of Speiser's presumption to link the issues of economic democracy, ideology and the nuclear arms race. His paper is illuminating in its examination of the interrelationship of these three phenomena. It also provides a useful point of reference to what follows.

Kenneth Krough describes himself as a retired bureaucrat. He worked as an official of the US Department of Agriculture for 24 years, first as a speech writer and finally as Assistant Administrator of the Foreign Agricultural Service. Since his college days he has been involved in developing a new and more realistic concept of social and political relationships. He is unfettered by traditional academic bias, giving a freshness to his essay. His views are critical of the left/right framework of ideology and his contribution is a revolutionary perspective for viewing social systems. This perspective proves valuable in examining the arguments engendered by the contest question.

Paul Grenier's essay provides a detailed image of the Soviet power elite as well as the dominant value systems supporting the elites within both of the superpowers. He has recently received two master's degrees from Columbia University, where he studied at the Harriman Institute for Advanced Study of the Soviet Union. Currently, he is working with the Council on Economic Priorities in New York City. His essay goes behind the mask of ideology to suggest that if we want to end the nuclear nightmare, there must be nothing less than a transmutation of social values. In Grenier's view there are no quick solutions. Tinkering with the American economic system without more fundamental changes will not bring an end to the nuclear arms race.

The editor's paper indicates that economic injustice in America will likely worsen under any presumed future scenario. It also demonstrates that attempts to create economic democracy are very likely to be undermined by other crises. These other crises are excessive debt, pollution and population growth. Some tentative proposals to make the USOP concept more robust are offered. I am a professor of economics at Villanova University in Pennsylvania. I teach mainly mathematics, but would describe myself as a student of comparative economic systems.

My concern is with the economic systems of tomorrow, and I have spent my academic life researching those forces which will shape tomorrow's economies.

John Sedlak is an ordained Roman Catholic priest for the Diocese of Greensburg, Pennsylvania. He holds a bachelor of science degree in psychology and a master of divinity degree. Prior to studying for the priesthood, Father Sedlak worked for more than three years as a technical information specialist for the US Defense Mapping Agency in Washington D.C. Presently assigned as a parochial vicar to the Blessed Sacrament Cathedral, he also serves on the diocesan Peace and Justice Commission and works closely with the local St. Vincent de Paul Society, a lay organization ministering to the indigent. His interest in social issues is reflected in his essay which emphasizes the need to consider the value of work in any reform proposal. Suggestions he offers are well thought out and extend the USOP concept in an important direction.

The final paper in this volume was written by Larry Marshall. He makes his living as a telecommunications engineer in Reno, Nevada, but is a political activist at heart. Up until the Democratic National Convention of 1984, where he was on the platform committee as Nevada's representative for Gary Hart, he described himself as being "radically anti-military." Rather than go through life being passively indignant over the world's injustice, he has decided to take a more active course. His paper is a summary of the progress he has made. It too is sobering, for it implies that creating world peace demands a solution encompassing all the major issues of our time as well as the concerns of all groups involved. Marshall proposes an approach for deriving such a "synergistic solution" and affirms the results of this contest as part of the first required step.

There were many other thoughtful essays submitted in the contest. Many of these the reader will be introduced to in this book through the editor's commentaries. It was impossible to include them all. The editor sought to select complete essays and excerpts which would help the reader to understand the complexity of the essay contest question as well as the complexity of the answers to it.

Every attempt has been made to present and comment on the essays in the spirit of pure discovery. Like many of the essayists, the editor believes that constructive answers to the essay contest question lie not with the materialistic, reductionistic thinking of the past, but rather with the holistic thinking of tomorrow.

II.

ECONOMIC REFORM FOR HUMANITY'S GREATEST STRUGGLE

by

Jon D. Wisman[1]

Humanity may have very little time to get its act together. As we all know, and struggle every day to forget, we are as close as 30 minutes from the end of our species' history. Little it would seem is being done to increase our survival chances. Indeed, our greatest commitment of brains and money is to the generation of ever new military technologies, insuring both a decrease in our survival likelihood and a further shortening of those last 30 minutes.

It is because of this frightening scenario that Stuart Speiser's recent pathbreaking book, *How to End the Nuclear Nightmare*, is so highly welcomed.[2] It is pathbreaking on two counts: It attempts to relate the issue of US-Soviet hostilities to economic institutions, and it suggests a radical measure we might take to reduce these hostilities.

Speiser's argument runs as follows. The crux of the problem of US-Soviet hostilities is to be found in ideology: "the clash between Marxism and capitalism is the root cause of Soviet-American enmity."[3] These ideological differences stem from the fact that our economic systems differ. We cannot change the Soviet system. Therefore, we should transform capitalism with what Speiser calls his SuperStock plan to make the ownership of capital more equal, such that our system is more in conformity with Marxist ideology. As Speiser puts it:

> By delivering MOP ["means of production," especially capital] ownership directly to the people through [SuperStock], we can fulfill the central goal of Marxism—ending the exploitation of the non-owning class . . . [and] with MOP ownership in the United States socialized via SuperStock, the two systems will be as close to compatibility as they can get.[4]

According to the SuperStock plan, most American households would wind up with $100,000 worth of non-voting stock in "our 2,000 major 'blue-chip' corporations."[5] These stocks would be purchased with government-backed loans which would be repaid with the stocks' dividends. Actually, for Speiser this plan would be a good idea anyway since "[i]n the broadest sense, both our domestic and international crises stem from one economic root—inequitable distribution of capital ownership and income."[6] These crises, combined with the perceived injustice of capitalism's distribution of capital and income, serve to make Marxism more attractive and thus pose additional threats to American ideals.

Unfortunately, in spite of the urgent importance of the subject Speiser addresses, his argument is not fully tenable. He has misspecified the problem, and this has led him to a policy recommendation which is inadequate to the task of reducing US-Soviet hostilities. He is mistaken in viewing ideological differences as the "root" cause of US-Soviet hostilities. These ideological differences, rather than being root causes, are instead the means of generating, maintaining and justifying the hostilities. Speiser appears not to grasp that the function of ideology is to legitimate. Consequently, it is unlikely that his SuperStock reform of capitalism would reduce US-Soviet hostilities. Indeed, it is equally possible that a narrowing of real differences between US and Soviet economic systems might actually heighten the need for political powers to engage in a form of ideological warfare which exaggerates the remaining differences. For instance, if the US economic system were made more egalitarian and hence more attractive, Soviet leadership might feel compelled to exaggerate further both the ideological differences and the extent of the US threat in order to justify their political power.

Yet at times Speiser seems keenly aware of the manner in which ideology is used as an instrument of control. For instance, note the following passage:

> Here we have the very crux of the problem: the Kremlin leaders *can-not* seek peace with capitalism in its present form if they wish to maintain their power, because that power is based squarely on an antagonistic relationship with capitalism. For the Soviets, ideology *must* take precedence over all other considerations.[7]

Presumably, for Speiser the crucial phrase in the above passage is "in its present form," suggesting that his SuperStock plan might make a difference, and at another point in his book Speiser is very close to recognizing that ideological differences may not correspond to real differences:

> So there we have it: 6 per cent (or less) in the USSR and 6 per cent (or less) in the US derive substantial benefits from ownership of the MOP. Thus, at the very moment in history when capitalism and communism are engaged in a death struggle arising from their differing ownership ideologies, it is plain that neither system produces substantial socialization of the income derived from MOP ownership.[8]

Ironically, to the extent that this comparison is true, Speiser's Super-Stock plan for making capital ownership more equal in the US would appear to make our system actually *less* similar to that of the Soviets.

Nevertheless, although Speiser's analysis is faulty, he is correct in suggesting that the problem of ideology must be addressed. He is also correct in proposing that the most effective step we can take toward reducing the threat of annihilation is to reform our economic system. However, because he has misunderstood the social function of ideology, the economic reform that he suggests is not quite what is required.

In this essay I will attempt to carry Speiser's work forward. The analysis will begin by examining the social function of ideology so as to reveal why it cannot be correctly viewed as the root cause of US-Soviet hostilities. The source of human vulnerability to warlike behavior will then be examined. It will be seen that although in the past this vulnerability abetted the evolution and survival of our species, it now threatens to bring human history to an end. The subsequent section will argue that our best hope lies in creating institutions which socialize humans to be self-reliant, critically self-aware and hence ever conscious of their susceptibility to ideologies which exploit warlike behavior.

The final section will suggest how we might implement the most promising reform of contemporary capitalism for habituating humans to be self-reliant and self-reflective. Like Speiser's proposed reform, it will result in more equal ownership of the means of production. However, it will go beyond Speiser's proposal by arguing that it is not ownership itself which is of principal importance. Instead it is the control of the means of production. Those in control must be responsible, they must make decisions, they must rely upon themselves and be ever critical of themselves. The proposal entails nothing more radical, nor less reasonable, than that workers must be placed in control of their own tools.

Beneath Ideology

Rivalry between political entities has always been expressed in terms of ideological differences. These differences have included depicting the members of other groups as not actually or fully human, viewing them as godless or seeing them as advocates of barbarian social institutions. Furthermore, members of rival political entities typically believe that their ideological differences are the root reason for hostilities. But are they? An answer to this question requires an understanding of the social function of ideology: Why does ideology exist?

At the most general level, ideology serves two related functions: it makes sense out of reality by providing a degree of coherence, and it serves as a guide for human behavior. Ideology legitimates institutions and behavior and makes them "correct" or "appropriate." It has been argued—convincingly, I believe—that humans must of necessity provide legitimation for their reality. As Peter Berger has put it, there "is a human craving for meaning that appears to have the force of instinct. Men are congenitally compelled to impose a meaningful order upon reality."[9]

Ideology thus can serve as a glue uniting a group or nation of people. However, within any given society institutions and behavior do not benefit all members equally. So, at a more specific level, ideology serves to legitimate, rationalize or render correct or appropriate institutions and behavior which further the cause of specific interests, possibly to the detriment of specific others, or even to a society as a whole.

All of this does not, of course, mean that ideology is without causal force. Indeed, quite the opposite is true. Ideology can motivate and guide humans to extraordinary feats. Yet although ideology is necessary and might be powerful, its specific content is itself caused. Consequently, exploitative or dangerous ideologies cannot be effectively eliminated or even tamed without addressing their causes.

It is for this reason, then, that Speiser's claim that "the clash between Marxism and capitalism is the root cause of Soviet-American enmity"[10] cannot be sustained. As ideologies, Marxism and capitalism are not themselves the source or cause of the hostilities between the Soviets and ourselves. Instead, these ideologies serve to make the hostilities legitimate. Consequently, to reduce the ideological distance between Marxism and capitalism without addressing what it is that these ideologies actually legitimate would not bring us closer to peace. What would likely occur is that either the remaining differences would take on greater importance or new ideologies would arise to take their place. History suggests that ideological distance is not overly important.

At times Speiser seems quite clear on this point. For instance, he notes that: "when France elected a socialist government in 1981 and embarked on large-scale nationalization of MOP ownership, their relations with the Soviets did not improve. In fact, Socialist [President] Mitterand moved further away from the USSR than had his capitalist predecessors, and he also vowed to build up France's nuclear deterrent."[11] Speiser goes on to note the hostility between China and the USSR as well as that between Vietnam and Cambodia. He then suggests that SuperStock might still work "because the case of the United States and the Soviet Union is a unique one"[12] due to the fact that they can totally destroy each other. However, Speiser has merely asserted, not demonstrated, that given this uniqueness SuperStock would be effective.

History has amply demonstrated that rival interests are capable of exaggerating the most minute ideological differences into mammoth proportions. For instance, the commonality of claiming allegiance to Marxism has not diminished Sino-Soviet hostilities. Both World Wars were principally among capitalist countries. Both Iran and Iraq adhere to Islam. The brutality of the countless conflicts between Catholics and Protestants since the Reformation do not seem to have been limited by a common belief in Christ. Nor does ideological distance stand in the way of peace, as our cooperation with the Soviet Union during World War II clearly demonstrates.

It would appear, then, that ideology is more a symptom than a cause of hostilities. It is a social product created to provide unity and justify hostility. Where humans have cause or might benefit from a hostile stance toward others, they can be counted upon to generate a set of reasons—an ideology—to provide meaning and justification for such hostility.

But why is such ideology so frequently found in human history? Are humans naturally warlike? It is to this question that our attention must now turn.

Vulnerability to Warlike Behavior

A great number of ethologists and biologists have extrapolated from their studies of animal behavior that all animals, humans included, are innately aggressive and hence warlike.[13] Darwin and others since have suggested that the very evolution of human intelligence is linked to the pervasiveness of warfare in the human experience.[14]

Still other students of human behavior suggest that humans are not genetically destined to be warlike. For instance, Richard Leakey and Roger Lewin argue that although "war is an outrageously successful activity . . . [and] an advantageous pursuit in a material world . . . it is a product of cultural invention, not a fundamental biological instinct."[15] Clearly, at the current stage of research the evidence is not yet compelling enough to generate scientific consensus as to whether humans are naturally destined to fight. In his highly respected textbook David P. Barash puts the issue as follows: "It is pointless to debate whether human beings are innately aggressive, especially because genetic and experiential factors are so intimately involved in the determination of such behavior."[16]

However, whether warlike behavior is a biological or a cultural product, one thing seems clear: evidence suggests that war and warlike behavior have been an ever-present part of the human experience. From both economic and evolutionary perspectives, this is not surprising. From an economic vantage point, in a world of scarcity it is under-standable that social groups would struggle against each other, perhaps war with each other, for control or possession of limited resources (hunting and gathering territories, cultivable land, etc.). From an evolutionary vantage point, those groups which were most successful in increasing their command over scarce resources would have a survival advantage which would permit them to increase their populations. This is why, of course, many students of human biology believe it likely that humans have been genetically selected for warlike behavior; the most successful fighters would best survive to pass their genes on to the future. Opponents to this view suggest that since fighting is only one of several ways of increasing command over scarce resources, it is specific cultural conditions which determine whether people will exhibit warlike behavior.

In any event, because war—or the threat of war—poses a life-and-death struggle, it requires total commitment from group members. If this commitment is weak, the group will be at a severe disadvantage against an enemy group where greater cohesion exists. This cohesion appears to come forth spontaneously when groups are threatened, even when the threat emanates from forces or events not resulting from the hostility of others. Natural catastrophes, shipwrecks and even electrical "brown-outs," for example, seem to elicit spontaneous group cohesion.

But where the threat is protracted, ideology can serve as a powerful force for preserving group unity. It is especially during wars that individuals appear willing to sacrifice their more narrow self-interest (including their lives!) for the greater good of the whole. Ideology gives justification or meaning to these sacrifices. Individuals must believe that the cause is worth fighting and possibly dying for. From an evolutionary perspective, those groups least capable of generating individual commitment would be less successful in the struggle for scarce resources and thus their members would stand less chance of passing on their genes. Insofar as ideology helped cement this commitment, it served as a useful social instrument in the struggle for survival.

War—even between quite small groups—is also more successfully pursued the greater the degree of social coordination. During war, optimal social coordination requires a leader. This is because strategies must be instantaneously determined in response to the enemy's ever-changing strategies. There is rarely time for participatory decision making. Consequently, it is in the interest of an entire group under threat from outsiders to give full allegiance to a leader. It is for this reason that leaders rarely achieve the same high degree of loyalty from their followers as during periods of war. During war or the imminent threat of war, this almost total loyalty appears to come forth spontaneously. However, if the threat is protracted or not always clearly in evidence, then ideology can serve to maintain loyalty either by sustaining a sense of threat or by granting special powers to the leaders (e.g., divine status or divine rights).

However, the very fact that war, or the serious threat of war, enables leaders to command an unparalleled degree of respect and loyalty places an almost irresistible temptation constantly in front of them: they can benefit if they can convincingly keep alive a perception of a threat of external aggression. Needless to say, resorting to such a strategy to maintain loyalty and hence political power is highly risky. If members of the group perceive that the alleged threat is either not real or not sufficient to merit the cost, then the leader loses credibility and may in fact lose power. For instance, this appears to have been the experience of US leaders during the Vietnam War. Consequently, leaders can be expected to craft limited measures against another power or other powers which might provoke a limited or measured amount of real threat. However, this can lead to catastrophe if hostilities escalate uncontrollably and result in war.

Escalation to war is, then, an ever-present likelihood. Leaders of both groups must craft their actions so as to maximize their chances of retaining power. Hostilities must be met forcefully. A leader will be rejected if it is believed that he or she is permitting the enemy to push the group around. A leader cannot survive if thought to be "soft" on a perceived aggressive enemy.

It is, of course, obvious that the cost of a war between the US and the USSR is potentially infinite. Thus, sophisticated atomic weapons are often credited with effectively ending major wars. In fact, the infinite cost of a US-Soviet war makes it considerably more difficult for leaders to appeal to the external threat strategy. In recent times President Reagan has talked of surviving nuclear war. Was he, in doing so, creating more space in which he could play up the Soviet menace strategy? Also, do religious doctrines which hold forth the promise of an afterlife, or especially those which come close to celebrating a forthcoming apocalypse, also increase the potential for leaders to maintain aggressive warlike stances?

But beyond these reflections on current US trends, the more general case is that although the temptation to appeal to an external threat, or if necessary work toward actually generating such a threat, is constantly before leaders, the extent to which they in fact resort to such strategy varies significantly. It depends upon two factors: the difficulty of maintaining credibility concerning an external threat without provoking war, and the success of leaders in maintaining an economically successful order.

Threat Credibility: The Case of Soviet Paranoia

Since the Bolshevik revolution in 1917, Soviet leaders have found it relatively easy to maintain the loyalty of their followers by appealing to external enemies. In fact, the credibility of this threat has been so great that the Soviet people have tolerated rather extreme curtailment of their civil and political freedoms.

Since the very beginning of the Soviet experiment, the Western capitalist powers have obligingly assisted the Soviet leadership in maintaining its monopoly on political power. No sooner had the Bolsheviks taken power than the French, British and the US set out to topple their government, principally by arming and financing counter-revolutionaries. The ensuing policies in the Soviet Union were called

"War Communism," and they included a restriction of civil liberties and an increase in the concentration of political power at the top. Throughout the 1920s there was a perceived threat that the socialist experiment would be undone by hostile capitalist countries. So strongly did Stalin feel this that he announced in 1931: "We must make good this distance [to become a first-rate economic and political power] in ten years. Either we do so, or we shall go under."[17] Stalin's words were, of course, prophetic since 10 years later Hitler invaded the Soviet Union.

The Russian people had suffered greatly during World War I, but that suffering was pale in comparison with the horrid costs of World War II—20 to 25 million Soviet people died as a result of that war. The Soviet fear of external aggression had not been unjustified, and it was that fear which had successfully legitimized a suspension of civil liberties, rule by an elite clique and a sacrifice of consumer welfare for defense.

Unfortunately, World War II ended in such a way that Soviet leaders would find easy legitimation for their totalitarian powers. The US dropped nuclear bombs on the Japanese, even though it did not appear to be necessary to US victory. The Soviet leadership had it made: To justify their every action they had only to remind their people of that act as evidence of how ruthlessly inhumane the US can be in pursuit of its interests.

The 20th century has schooled the Soviet people in fear and the reality of its objects. Soviet leaders are in substantial measure dependent upon this fear to maintain the respect and loyalty of the Soviet people. This analysis suggests that our most effective contemporary stance toward the Soviet Union for reducing tensions would be to undertake those actions which suggest to the Soviet peoples that we are not intent upon destroying their society.

Economic Success

As noted above, appealing to an external threat to generate respect and loyalty is a risky strategy for leaders. If the threat is not credible, the strategy may backfire. If the strategy is carried too far, it may provoke war and ensuing catastrophe. Consequently, we would not expect leaders to play heavily upon the external threat theme if all is going well. The external threat card is their ace in the hole, albeit a risky one to use.

Short of its success in providing defense and domestic law and order, the most important criterion for judging leadership is its ability to maintain material or economic prosperity. If members of a society feel that their material condition is secure or improving, they are likely to be strongly supportive of their political leaders. Thus, leaders of strong economies are more likely to reap the respect and loyalty of their followers. By contrast, if under their leadership material well-being declines or is threatened, leaders are likely to face a legitimacy crisis. And it is during such legitimacy crises that leaders will be most tempted to play their trump card: to struggle to rally support by showing prowess against external threats.

An interesting hypothesis is that a significant correlation may exist between macroeconomic dysfunction and bellicosity. World War II grew out of the worst economic depression in the history of capitalism. The peace movement and detente came forth during the extraordinary worldwide economic prosperity of the 1960s. When economic progress began to falter in the 1970s, detente began to be drowned out by rattling sabers. Note also that during the 1960s there was widespread confidence in governments' ability to use Keynesian tools to insure macroeconomic stability, whereas during the late 1970s and early 1980s there was a resurfacing of laissez-faire doctrine which argued that governments are essentially powerless to stabilize economies. These casual observations do not, of course, test the hypothesis. Extensive research would be needed to do that.[18]

In any event, throughout recorded history economies have periodically fallen upon hard times. In predominantly agricultural societies this was usually due to the vagaries of climate.[19] In modern times, by contrast, economic dysfunction is principally due to the relative unresponsiveness and inflexibility of our economic institutions in face of ever more rapid technological change and ever greater worldwide interdependency.

Thorstein Veblen called this tendency of more static social institutions to hold back the dynamism of technological change "cultural lag." A similar theme had been set forth by Marx in terms of social relations of production retarding forces of production. More recently, Mancur Olson has discussed this general theme, again in quite different terms, in his *The Rise and Decline of Nations*.[20] It would, of course, be a mistake to attempt to slow technological change or the growth of interdependency. Both provide for the growth and spread of abundance and thus the enhanced well-being of humanity. Furthermore, the growth of interdependency also serves the long-run interest of peace.

Nevertheless, a relatively high level of macroeconomic stability must be maintained if for no other reason than that when an economy falters, leaders' fitness to rule is placed in question. This, of course, increases the chance that they will attempt to divert attention by playing up an external threat. Today the exercise of this strategy places the entire human species in mortal danger. Consequently, we must struggle to craft our economic institutions for flexible responsiveness to change so as to insure better prosperity and decrease the probability that leaders resort to bellicosity.

The threat need not, of course, be external, although it is considerably more difficult to conjure up a convincing internal threat when one is not truly there. However, Hitler's success in convincing Germans that domestic Jews and Communists were not only responsible for economic dysfunction but that they posed a more general danger as well demonstrates that it can be done. A similar phenomenon also occurred in the Soviet Union. In a recent article Walter Laqueur argues that "as far as [the common people] were concerned, the show trials provided an explanation of why so many things had gone wrong inside the Soviet Union, why the economy was still in poor shape: it was all the fault of the enemy from within, the saboteurs and the wreckers."[21]

Regrettably, there is no way to protect fully against economic dysfunction in today's increasingly complex world. Economic dysfunction is bound to occur from time to time even with the best leadership. And unfortunately, leaders will be tempted to deflect attention from these crises and rally support for themselves by appealing to a foreign menace. Therefore, humanity must learn better to cope with this strategy. We need institutions which socialize members of society to be self- reliant and highly critical, both of leaders and of themselves. We must become capable of fully grasping our vulnerability to warlike behavior.

The Need for Economic Reform

America celebrates the concept of democracy. Yet, surprisingly, it does so only in the political realm, not in the economic. In the economic realm it accepts the principle of the vertical structure of authority, the very principle that is at the heart of all totalitarian societies. Nine out of every ten American workers take orders from above—they are bossed about. The ratio is approximately the reverse of what was the case 200 years ago when our principles of democracy were being formulated into law. Stanley Lebergott has estimated that as late as 1850 about 70 per cent of the free work force was self-employed.[22] Of course, it was the dominance of agriculture and the small scale of manufacturing technology that permitted most individuals to be their own bosses.

Because today American workers no longer own or control the tools and resources with which they work, they must bow unquestioningly to the authority of the owners or their agents; they must take and execute orders uncritically.

Many social thinkers have argued against the unsatisfactory nature of division between capital and labor. For example, over 140 years ago, John Stuart Mill wrote:

> I cannot think that [workers] will be permanently contented with the condition of labouring for wages as their ultimate state. To work at the bidding and for the profit of another, without any interest in the work—the price of their labour being adjusted by hostile competition, one side demanding as much and the other paying as little as possible—is not, even when wages are high, a satisfactory state to human beings of educated intelligence, who have ceased to think themselves naturally inferior to those whom they serve.[23]

Mill's point is more poignant today than ever. Since the overwhelming majority of Americans are more involved in the economic than the political realm, their acculturation is predominantly in subservience rather than self-reliance and democracy. Because they must take orders from above, because responsible decision making is done by somebody else, they are not optimally trained in using their creative and critical faculties.

It is an affront to human dignity to be bossed about, and consequently the hierarchical, non-democratic nature of work in America merits reform on this ground alone. But in the face of the danger of nuclear war, this reform takes on special urgency. The non-democratic nature of work increases our vulnerability to war in two ways: First, it increases the potential for macroeconomic dysfunction. Second, by making Americans both less critical and more dependent on the judgment of others, it increases the possibility that political leaders will be successful in gaining respect and loyalty by exaggerating the Soviet menace.

The issue of macroeconomic dysfunction requires further explanation. The fact that workers neither own nor control the means of production creates the potential for what might be called "capital-labor strife." Capital-labor strife results when the interests of the owners of capital and those of workers are at odds. For instance, the cost of creating a safer workplace may reduce profits; new technology may displace workers; work rules may increase jobs at the cost of lower profits; relocated plants may increase profits, but harm specific workers and their communities. All of these conflicts between the interests of capital and labor reduce productivity and hence the ability of American industry to survive foreign competition.

These conflictual interests are also expressed politically, and this has become especially dysfunctional in economies suffering both relatively high unemployment and inflation. When political parties partial to the interests of workers are elected, stimulative Keynesian policies are set in motion to reduce unemployment. An undesirable consequence, however, is that inflation tends to worsen. Worsened inflation paves the way for the election of parties more representative of the interests of capital that use restrictive Keynesian tools to fight inflation. But the cost of this tends to be higher unemployment, which improves the election chances of the political parties with greater worker representation.

The consequence is that the interests of capital and labor seesaw in political power, alternately hitting the brakes and then the accelerator, thereby creating chronic macroeconomic instability and slowing the growth of economic prosperity. (This suggests that perhaps the modern business cycle should be viewed as more a political than economic phenomenon. The argument that the business cycle is in fact a political cycle has been set forth by economists on both the right and left.)[24] As noted above, when leaders are unable to maintain respect and loyalty by delivering economic security and prosperity, they are more tempted to play their trump card of arousing the spector of external aggression.

The reform which is essential, then, is one which reunites workers with their tools. It is fortuitous that this reform would be welcomed even without its potential for reducing the threat of nuclear annihilation. It promises fuller democracy and greater human dignity. Uniting workers with their tools would overcome capital-labor strife, and would entail both greater productivity and greater prosperity. In addition, it would dramatically increase the ability of our economy to respond to technological change and foreign competition, and thus reduce the likelihood of economic dysfunction. Finally, it would help to socialize Americans to be democratic, self-reliant and critically minded. A study by Lorraine B. Blank has found that workers who own and control their own firms tend to become more active both in local politics and in voluntary organizations.[25] A proposal for carrying out this reform is outlined in the section which follows.

The Specific Proposal

The average American worker works with approximately $60,000 worth of plant and equipment.[26] The proposal is to use government-backed loans and incentives to enable workers to purchase, and thus control, the tools and resources with which they work. It should be noted that this would not represent a radical departure for the US political system. At the founding of our nation most workers did own and control their means of production. And since 1974 the US government has passed several pieces of legislation to encourage worker ownership through Employee Stock Ownership Plans (ESOPs).

The following proposal departs from the ESOP program in only two ways: First, it would carry out the transfer of ownership in a relatively short period of time. Second, it would require that voting rights (decision-making responsibility) accompany ownership.

The proposal would work in much the same way that government-insured mortgages assist certain people in purchasing homes. The principal different is that, initially, purchase of corporate equity would need to be staggered over a number of years to minimize distortions in credit and equity markets.[27] Thus, suppose the intent is to transfer full ownership within a 10-year period and that equity per worker is $60,000. During each year of a 10-year phase-in period, workers would take out government-backed loans of $6,000 from conventional private lenders at market rates of interest to purchase common stock equity in the company where they work. Each of these $6,000 loans would have a 30-year payback period (exactly as with a 30-year home mortgage).

At first blush it might appear that $60,000 (the approximate average value of the tools and resources with which the average worker works) would be too great a financial burden for the average US household. However, this figure is considerably below the average price of an American home (over $80,000), and approximately 65 per cent of all American households own, or are in the process of buying, their own homes. Furthermore, whereas capital ownership yields income which may be used to pay off worker-owner loans, home ownership typically does not yield money income.

Thus, at the end of the 10-year period, each worker would have voting control of his or her equal share of the company. Since World War II the average annual return to corporate equity in the US has varied between 9.7 per cent in the worst years to 15.5 per cent in the best. In general, then, if retained earnings were paid out as dividends, they should, on average, take care of the loan payoff. However, to better insure that the payoff not be onerous, as well as to further encourage this ownership transformation, dividends distributed to workers for shares on which they are still paying off loans could be free of personal income tax. Additionally, all retained earnings distributed to workers as dividends could be free of corporate income taxes. This latter inducement would mean that a firm entirely owned and controlled by its workers—this being the social ideal—would pay no corporate income tax.

Two amendments to this proposal could be added to address the problems of plant closings and unemployment. Plant closings and the consequent destruction of communities might be arrested by offering government-backed loans to threatened workers for the full purchase price of plants which are about to be closed or which are dramatically reducing their work forces. Capital-labor strife would be overcome, and thus the workers, no longer fearing that absentee owners would be the sole beneficiaries of their sacrifices, could go about doing what would be necessary to save their plants (e.g., cut their own wages, speed up the work process, innovate, etc.). Since such industries are obviously in quite unhealthy condition, the loan payback might be scheduled not to begin until after the end of a reasonable recuperation period of, say, five or six years.

Chronic unemployment might be eliminated by offering a firm a $10,000 training fee to take on a new worker-owner. This would be a long-run savings to society since, once placed, these new worker-owners would not likely return to the rolls of the unemployed. Robert B. Reich has reported that "[e]very 1 per cent increase in the jobless rate costs roughly $75 billion in lost production of goods and services, $25 billion in lost taxes, and $5 billion in unemployment compensation."[28] From this we can calculate that on average one additional unemployed individual costs the nation about $68,000 per year in lost output alone ($75 billion divided by 1 per cent unemployment, or 1.1 million workers). Compared to this figure, a $10,000 bribe to a firm to take on an unemployed worker, especially if permanently removing the worker from the unemployment rolls would appear as a very good bargain.

Although space does not permit a full elaboration of this proposal, a number of brief points might be made for clarity. First, privately held businesses could elect not to sell ownership shares to employees. They would, of course, have to make employment adequately attractive such that their workers would not choose to become worker-owners elsewhere. The government could only lose money in cases where a company is forced to file for bankruptcy, being without adequate assets after all debts are covered, or where for whatever reason a worker defaults on payments. Third, because a company might fail through no fault of the employees, workers must be given more than one chance. But taxpayers must also be protected from irresponsible behavior. Thus, workers applying for a second or third government-secured loan to purchase their share of equity in new firms might be required to come forth with a down payment of, say, 10 per cent. Fourth, it is likely that workers would retain much of the present management personnel. Such managers might or might not become owner-workers themselves. The major difference is that managers would be selected by and answerable to workers as opposed to absentee owners. Fifth, non-workers might be permitted part ownership in worker-owned firms through the purchase of non-voting stock shares. Finally, it is unlikely that this proposal would increase either the size of government or fiscal deficits. In fact, by eliminating capital-labor strife, some current government regulations (e.g., those concerning workplace health and safety) might no longer be required. More highly motivated worker-owners would be more highly productive, raising national income and hence government revenues, while the reduction in unemployment would increase tax receipts and reduce the need for government income support programs.

I do not mean to suggest that the plan offered here would solve all our problems. Indeed, there are a number of somewhat new, although not unmanageable, problems which worker ownership poses. However, I believe that movement toward worker ownership and control of the means of production constitutes the most progressive direction which we might take for improving our material condition, increasing our freedom and avoiding our self-destruction.

Concluding Reflections

Speiser examines a number of proposals for worker ownership and then rejects them in favor of his SuperStock plan.[29] In his book, however, he has not examined a proposal for moving toward worker ownership (such as the one offered here), which is as comprehensive as his SuperStock plan and which requires as little government participation. But far more important, Speiser has failed to understand that the critical issue facing humanity is not merely one of material inequalities. Instead, it is the question of human development, of individual self-determination and self-reliance.

Although Speiser's SuperStock plan would create greater wealth and income equality, it would not directly change the everyday existence of most Americans. The major consequence of his plan is that most Americans would become absentee owners of a chunk of blue-chip America. However, they would not possess any greater control over their work-a-day lives. They would still work within authoritarian institutions, taking orders from above. Their work-a-day lives would not call upon them to practice democracy and responsibility in decision making. In fact, Speiser's SuperStock plan would not even permit them to vote their blue-chip holdings.

Speiser argues that "SuperStock is consistent with America's greatest traditions." I do not believe that this is true. Although absentee ownership has grown dramatically since the Civil War, it represents a divorce of ownership from responsibility, and it could be argued that this is strikingly contrary to "America's greatest traditions." At the turn of the century, there was widespread reaction among social thinkers to the divorce of ownership and responsibility. Especially notable were R. H. Tawney in England and Thorstein Veblen in the United States.[30]

Speiser also argues that SuperStock would give us "an American form of capitalism that is truly democratic . . ."[31] But in the US democracy usually means greater equality only in the sense of an equal sharing of responsibility in decision making. SuperStock would not increase democracy in this sense of the word. Indeed, it is not fully clear what democracy means for Speiser. For instance, his suggestion that SuperStock be non-voting ownership is based upon his lack of confidence that workers would be responsible owners.[32] This is reminiscent of the 19th century rationale in Europe for not extending suffrage to the working class.

These differences between SuperStock and the plan offered here are crucial for the subject in question: "How can we, without adopting socialism or giving up our treasured freedoms, modify American capitalism to make it more equitable and reduce the level of ideological conflict with the Soviet Union so as to make possible an end to the nuclear nightmare?" It is not by making our economic systems more like that of the Soviet Union that ideological conflict will be reduced. As argued above, ideological warfare does not depend upon the extent of real differences. Instead, ideological warfare serves to legitimate political power.

The strategy which we must pursue is threefold: We must reduce the perception within the Soviet Union that we are out to destroy their "evil empire." Second, we must create economic institutions which greatly reduce macroeconomic dysfunction, since this increases the temptation of our leaders to play upon the theme of an external threat. Third, we must transform our social institutions so that they can acculturate Americans to be as self-reliant and self-critical as possible. Only an independent, self-reliant and self-critical population can serve as a sufficient defense against our vulnerability to ideology and warlike behavior.

No matter how instrumental war or warlike behavior may have been in the evolution of the human species, today both are irrational in the extreme—they threaten the species with extinction. Our hope lies in our capacity to grasp the full nature of this irrationality. It may appear fortuitous that the ideal proposal for doing this and thus for moving toward more secure peace is also the one which most dramatically enhances human freedom and democracy. However, it is not in fact merely a coincidence. It is human intelligence which brought us to this frighteningly advanced state where we are poised to self-destruct. It is only human intelligence which can move us beyond this dangerous point in our evolution. Human intelligence stands the greatest chance of advancement where humans are free, self-reliant and democratically called upon to participate in making decisions. Consequently, the greatest single reform of capitalism for moving toward an end of the nuclear nightmare is to transfer peaceably and democratically to workers themselves the ownership and control of the tools and resources with which they work.

Editor's Comments

Jon Wisman has made several valuable contributions in addressing the central question with which this volume is concerned. He argues that the ideological differences between the United States and the Soviet Union are not the cause of the superpower conflict, but rather a means of sustaining that conflict. He then examines human vulnerability to warlike behavior, noting that while the vulnerability aided the evolution and survival of our species in the past, it now threatens us with extinction.

Our best hope in Wisman's view is to create institutions that will help us to become more self-reliant, more critically self-aware and more conscious of our susceptibility to ideologies that exploit warlike behavior. His chosen vehicle for accomplishing these goals is worker ownership and control of the means of production.

Several other essays submitted to the contest argue for the worker self-management model. Rather than a top-down approach to economic reform, Jerome Rabow and Lynn Sappington present a bottom-up strategy in their paper, "Modified Speiser Plan." This strategy is centered on worker-ownership and would test the USOP concept for eventual full-scale implementation.

Contribution by Jerome Rabow and Lynn Sappington

Although Speiser's plan is a logical and sensible one, there would be much opposition from various sectors of society to this proposal. Individuals who doubt that such a program could really be carried out would be skeptical and might organize against a plan that looks like a give-away. A modified smaller scale version of the Speiser plan would, therefore, more likely be acceptable. This plan could serve as a type of testing ground for the central idea that people who are gainfully employed, with a sense of security about their future, will tend to have a stake in the world and tend not to support a nuclear war. The project itself would follow most, if not all, of Speiser's ideas, with the goal of testing and validating its promise as a full-scale venture. . . .

A search must be made for a community that wants to start a new business or branch, or for a plant or business that wants to develop new technology or new products. This might perhaps be a town with acute or chronic unemployment that seeks to reduce it through business expansion. Such a community *must* be mixed in order to alleviate favoring any sector of American society. Such a community should be divided among members of different age groups, gender, religions and political affiliation. In this way all members of society would be able to identify with the community and endorse expansion of the plan. Many communities all over America would be interested in such an offer. Communities are always seeking new industry. Under the SuperStock Plan, members of the community who want to work in the new business venture would apply. The hiring practices would favor those who are not gainfully employed. These new employees would participate in a profit-sharing plan and receive stock in the company so that ownership of the venture is maintained by employees. The profits would be divided among the employees as salary and as payback to the Federal government. The payment of dividends would start immediately on an annual basis. Owners of stock would not be permitted to sell their stock. Only termination and death would provide grounds for the sale of stock. Replacement of employment would be given to the deceased member's family with the passing on of stock ownership.[33]

The authors argue that the support necessary for the eventual adoption of a USOP would grow if we begin with community-level worker-managed enterprises. Given that workers own their means of production and begin to receive dividends immediately, strong grassroots support might well develop for a USOP.

Like Wisman, Francis Kingen points to economic instability as a contributing factor underlying tensions between the superpowers in his paper, "World Peace Through Monetary Systems Change."

Contribution by Francis Kingen

The first step in destroying the stability of the monetary system was the introduction of the concept known as fractional reserve banking. A failure to recognize the objectives of monetary systems in modern democratic societies has led to monetary system modifications that exacerbate economic problems rather than solve them.

The final blow to stability in the system was delivered by President Nixon in 1971 when he abandoned the agreement the US had made with member nations of the International Monetary Fund, to exchange gold bullion for US dollars when requested by member nations. This action destroyed the unit standard and the final connection between the issue of paper money and the creation of wealth. . . .

We must not only change the way our economy functions to decrease our conflict with that of the USSR, but change it so as to prevent the degeneration of our economy, and provide an example for the threatened economies of Third World societies with which they may avoid a condition conducive to superpower intervention. If the US fails to cure its economic woes, the economies of a major portion of the Third World are in jeopardy. . . .

The essence of the system I propose requires changes in laws governing the Federal Reserve System, and the banking services of the nation. These changes would require that the process for handling savings accounts be separated from accounts consisting of newly created money (approximately $300 billion in 1984). New money must not be loaned but issued to account for new wealth being brought into the economy from the economic system's interface with the environment. The new money is to bear no interest. The system automatically removes the money from the monetary system to account for consumption. This process is applicable to any economy from right to left without changing the basic philosophy of any government.[34]

Although Kingen presents only one of many potential world monetary reform proposals, the basic point of his essay is that the present lack of a stable monetary system creates a crisis-prone world economic environment which intensifies capitalist/Communist rivalry. We may infer from this that it will take more than a national worker-management movement or a USOP to create macroeconomic stability.

Worker self-management is not a new and untried concept. It has been the economic centerpiece in Yugoslavia since 1950, and there are numerous examples of this type of enterprise in the United States. Unfortunately, many of the worker self-management enterprises in the US have failed—not because of an inherent flaw in the concept, but due to the fact that the previous stockowners typically relinquish control only when it appears that the business is doomed. Given these circumstances, it is not surprising that worker ownership is still a relatively limited phenomenon in American economic life.

There have been several notable exceptions to this pattern in the recent past that have received mass media attention and that may turn the tide of perception. Current experiments include, along with many unmentioned small businesses, Eastern Airlines, Weirton Steel, W.L. Gore and Associates, Publix Supermarkets, US Sugar and P.I.E. Nationwide. Of these, Eastern Airlines and Weirton Steel have both turned around unprofitable businesses and received national acclaim. Research by Corey Rosen, executive director of the National Center for Employee Ownership, as well as research conducted by the New York Stock Exchange, have found that firms which had at least 10 per cent worker ownership had higher profits and grew faster than other firms. If the accumulation of supportive evidence continues to build, the worker self-management model would be expected to spread more quickly and more widely in the future.

In most cases employee ownership will increase worker incentives and enhance productivity, while reducing absenteeism, job turnover and alienation. Still, worker self-management is no panacea. Studies of worker-owned enterprises in Yugoslavia have shown certain negative facets. These firms seek to maximize the long-term income per employee. Due to this, the firm is unlikely to hire new workers unless it can be clearly determined that their contribution will greatly exceed their cost. Thus, offsetting to a certain degree the capacity of these firms to enhance macroeconomic growth is a tendency to minimize employment opportunity in the worker self-managed firm itself.

Superior efficiency and hard work is not a guarantee of higher profits and higher income. Worker self-managed enterprises in mature or declining industries may find themselves faced with chronic problems in the marketplace they cannot overcome. For Yugoslav firms, in these types of industries it was found that workers were less willing to commit current income to investments, that efficiency and dedication deteriorated and that worker turnover increased.

In worker self-managed companies the design of the decision-making structure is problematic. The definition of such an enterprise leads to potential conflict between workers and their elected management. Authority is circular: workers dictate policy and are subordinate to the execution of their policies. This circular arrangement of authority may politicize workers on policy matters, taking time, energy and commitment from production.

Feeding internal confrontation are the differing objectives people bring with them to the workplace. For instance, young workers in a self-managed enterprise will tend to emphasize equal treatment among workers and investments which maximize long-term income. Older workers will tend to emphasize seniority and investments which maximize short-term income.

The best-run worker-managed company would be one which has well-educated employees with a high degree of economic sophistication. The employees would ideally come from a culture that emphasizes and builds on a tradition of participation. As Wisman points out, Americans' socialization tends toward subservience in the workplace, although hardly more so that in many other societies. We are forced to conclude that at this time, Americans are unprepared for the kind of participation a worker self-managed firm demands. The research conducted by Corey Rosen on workers in such American firms corroborates this view. Rosen found that given a choice between more money and more decision-making opportunity, workers almost always choose the money. He concludes that for a worker-owned firm in America to succeed today, it is more important for the managers than for the workers to support it.

All of the above-mentioned qualifications are meant to temper the readers' perception of the worker self-management model, not to negate it. The editor believes that this economic reform model attains more on several important levels than Speiser's USOP. It is also the editor's hope that some final vision of American economic reform will eventually emerge incorporating both concepts.

III

SOCIAL CHANGE AND THE LIMITS OF IDEOLOGY

Editor's Introduction

On one level, the core objection Karl Marx had to capitalism was the ownership of the means of production (MOP) by the small group of capitalists. His labor theory of value argues that the workers are ultimately the source of any commodity's value. Under capitalism, the prevailing institutions defining the ownership of capital channel the majority of extra income generated in the production process, above cost, to capitalists. Thus, the capitalist class lives on the sweat of the worker's brow. This Marx condemned as immoral.

His solution was to shift the ownership of the MOP from the small group of capitalists to the people in general. Since the capitalists sit in the seat of societal power, he concluded (at least in his *Manifesto*) that the only effective means to redefine the institution of ownership, to unseat the capitalists, was revolution.

As one digs more deeply into the works of Marx, one gets a better idea precisely why Marx condemned capitalism as immoral. He argued that human beings are molded by their environment, defined in large part by their relationship with the workplace. Under capitalism, Marx argued that separation of a person from ownership of the tools he uses violates his basic being. In Marx's words:

> Labor is, in the first place, a process in which both man and nature participate, and in which man of his own accord starts, regulates, and controls the material reactions between himself and nature . . . . By thus acting on the external world and changing it, he at the same time changes his own nature. He develops his slumbering powers . . . .[1]

In this vein it could be argued that on a more fundamental level Marx's primary objection to capitalism is based on the forced separation it engenders between workers and what and how they produce.

In the third volume of *Capital*, Marx (and presumably Friedrick Engels since he edited the book after Marx's death) made some interesting comments which caught Stuart Speiser's eye. In one particular passage Marx indicates that the joint-stock corporation could be used to help return ownership to the workers. After describing the credit system which exists under capitalism, he states:

> This credit system, since it forms the principal basis for the gradual transformation of capitalist private enterprise into capitalist joint-stock companies, presents in the same way the means for the gradual extension of cooperative enterprises on a more or less national scale. Capitalist joint-stock companies as much as cooperative factories should be viewed as transition forms from the capitalist mode of production to the associated one, simply that in the one case the opposition is abolished in a negative way, and in the other in a positive way.[2]

Speiser seizes upon this quotation to argue that a USOP is compatible with the teachings of Marx. A USOP would distribute the ownership of the majority of future capital to all Americans. Marx wanted the MOP socialized so everyone could share in the surplus value they create. The Marxist institution guaranteeing socialized ownership was the dictatorship of the proletariat; Speiser's institution guaranteeing socialized ownership would be a USOP.

Oskar Lange argued in his famous essay that the capitalist market mechanism was not strictly indigenous to capitalism and could be resurrected in various forms to make socialism operate more efficiently.[3] Speiser seems to continue in this tradition by claiming that the institutions defining ownership of capital are also not inherent or inseparable from capitalism. Furthermore, he implies that the existing institutional mechanism defining future ownership of capital can be successfully redefined without seriously disrupting efficiency or incentives.

We noted above that Marx's objection to capitalism was centered on two conditions—the inequitable distribution of ownership and the forced separation between workers and what and how they produce. A

USOP would address the inequitable distribution of ownership, but only partially the separation issue. The question we must ask is how much will the alienation of workers from the work process be reduced by giving them shares of a non-voting mutual fund with only dividends as a tangible benefit. Upon these reflections it could be decisively argued that Wisman's proposal to encourage universal worker ownership goes the greater distance toward attaining ideological compatibility. Widespread worker ownership would disseminate the MOP while directly uniting people with the environment in which they work.

Wisman's contention that Speiser had misspecified the ideological issue was echoed by many other essayists. The paper, "Survival Is Our Business" by James Mason, provides a good example of these recurring doubts.

> If SuperStock is to have any bearing on our relations with the Soviet Union, it can do so only if two of Mr. Speiser's assumptions are correct: that the most important area of conflict between the USA and the USSR is the ideological conflict between capitalism and Marxism; and that placing the means of production (MOP) in the hands of the American people will somehow resolve this ideological hostility.[4]

Experts disagree as to the role of ideology in the American-Soviet antagonism. In his 1980 book, *The Real War,* former President Richard Nixon says:

> What threatens the world is not theoretical "communism," not philosophical "Marxism," but rather an aggressive, expansionist totalitarian force that has adopted those names for an ideological fervor it has grafted onto the roots of tsarist expansionism and tsarist despotism![5]

And Freeman Dyson argues that: "We do not need to think alike in order to survive together on this planet. We need only to understand that it is possible to think differently and to respect each other's points of view!"[6]

These views are in contrast to those of Stuart Speiser who observes ". . . what we're fighting to protect is *capitalism.* What we're fighting to protect it from is the appeal of an *idea,* not necessarily Russian-style communism, but the Marxist ideology. And we fear its appeal largely because of the failings of our own capitalism."[7] Dyson, however, goes on to say:

> Ideology is obviously of signal importance—Marxism-Leninism is the wellhead of a fundamentally adversarial world view that casts the

Soviet Union and the Western capitalist powers on opposite sides of historical barricades.[8]

Former Ambassador to the Soviet Union, Foy Kohler, while arguing that the power of Soviet ideology is declining, observes: "The more the power of Marxist-Leninist ideology declines, the more frantically does the Kremlin leadership feel impelled to proclaim its validity and force its acceptance."[9] According to Robert G. Kaiser:

> Some future generation of Soviet leaders could decide—and may have good reason to decide—that history really is on the side of Marxism-Leninism, and that communism will conquer the world. If we in the Western world continue to mismanage our affairs, we will encourage the Russians to reach that conclusion.[10]

Ideology is obviously important, although perhaps not as basic as Speiser contends. We *can* reach agreements with the Soviets without resolving our ideological conflicts. It would obviously be easier to reach agreements if these conflicts could be eliminated.

Would SuperStock make capitalism and Marxism-Leninism more compatible? If the United States Congress should pass legislation putting SuperStock into effect, the Soviet Union might react in one of three ways: (a) treat it with indifference, (b) view it as a sign of weakness and be encouraged to undertake further adventures, or (c) see it as a sign of US desire for improved relations and seize the opportunity for meaningful negotiations.

Indifference is probably the least likely reaction. The Soviets study everything the United States does and attempt to decipher our motives and intentions. Their analysis may be wrong, but they are unlikely to be indifferent. We cannot, however, be guided by Soviet reaction in considering domestic legislation. To do so would mean that we have already surrendered to the Russians. As Speiser says:

> Since we cannot be certain that socializing American MOP ownership will end the nuclear nightmare, we must first make certain that SuperStock is worth doing on its own—that it will help the American economy rather than harm it, regardless of its ability to end the nuclear arms race.[11]

Another essayist, Kenneth Krough, contends that the standard rhetoric of ideology leads thinkers away from the essence of what is really going on. He argues that a different perspective revolving around the concept of societal maturation proves more enlightening in understanding the role ideological convergence plays in resolving in the nuclear nightmare. Along the way, Krough presents us with an informative history of the idea of using capital ownership to attain economic democracy.[12]

Making Universal Capitalism a Reality

by Kenneth K. Krough

Origins of Universal Capitalism

How can we modify American capitalism so as to (a) make it more equitable, (b) reduce the level of ideological conflict with the Soviet Union and (c) make possible an end to the nuclear nightmare?

A number of pioneer thinkers believe the answers to such questions have been available for decades. The answers, they insist, lie in the implementation of a new kind of economic system called "universal capitalism."

But after some 25 years of largely unsuccessful efforts to excite public interest in their proposals, they are reassessing their position:

- What has gone wrong?

- Why have such obvious remedies gone unacknowledged?

- What more needs to be done?

It would now appear that the answers to their queries lie not so much in the "what" of their proposals as in the "how." It is not the nuts and bolts of their proposals that may need attention so much as their conceptual approach to the problem as a whole. Making a reality of universal capitalism may involve a quite different type of struggle than they think.

Universal capitalism as such calls for a change in the "plumbing" of American capitalism. Instead of a plumbing system that automatically pipes the ownership of newly formed capital to the 5 per cent of Americans who already own most of US capital, the new system would pipe such ownership to the 95 per cent of Americans who own little or no capital. Such a modified system would broaden the base of American capital ownership—making capitalism "universal" among the American people as a whole without taking capital from established owners.

Louis O. Kelso, one of the pioneer advocates of universal capitalism, noted that most new capital is financed in such a way as to pay for itself out of its own earnings. If capital thus *pays for itself*— regardless of who eventually owns it—he reasoned that the eventual

new owners might as justifiably be those who own little or no capital as those who already are richly endowed. Indeed, he saw such a modification of capitalism as not only more equitable and just, but as a modification which would work much more effectively in an economic sense than capitalism does at present.

Profits from the expanded base of capital ownership would put additional purchasing power in the pockets of the very people—the people of society at large—on whom capitalist systems have always depended to buy the goods and services produced. Periodic market gluts and their attendant economic recessions would thus be reduced, and with the population as a whole receiving income from capital ownership, full employment, as such, would no longer be as crucial an issue as before. "Unemployment," Kelso explained, "is not so bad for those who can afford it."

Kelso published his theory of "universal capitalism" in *The Capitalist Manifesto,* a book he co-authored in 1958 with Mortimer J. Adler.[13] Since that time he has been joined by other pioneer advocates of universal capitalism—Norman Kurland, Patricia Hetter and Stuart Speiser among them—who have worked tirelessly to gain widespread recognition and support for the theory.

But widespread recognition and support for Kelso's theory of universal capitalism, as we have noted, has not come about. After more than 25 years, the theory has yet to be given serious consideration by the economics profession in general, and government hearings on the subject, while generally favorable, have had little substantive impact.

It is true that broadened capital ownership has made dramatic gains in the realm of employee stock ownership plans in recent years. Corey Rosen in a recently issued study reports that employee ownership is one of the fastest growing trends in American business with more than 10 million workers in more than 7,000 companies participating.[14] But Stuart Speiser notes that while most employee stock ownership plans have positive aspects, none are broad enough to serve as an effective instrument of universal capitalism. Most Americans, he points out, are self-employed, or work for companies whose stock is not traded publicly, or work for government or nonprofit organizations—or do not work at all. Thus, he concludes, employee ownership schemes do nothing to help the poor or the great majority of Americans who are not fortunate enough to be employed by blue-chip companies.[15]

So where do the advocates of universal capitalism go from here? What can be done to wake up the economics profession and the country at large to the validity of the Kelso theory? What is the key to the successful implementation of universal capitalism?

The Trap for Unconventional Ideas

Stuart Speiser believes that the threat of nuclear war can be used to shock the American people into recognition of the validity and necessity of universal capitalism. In his book, *How to End the Nuclear Nightmare,* he attempts to "harness all the energy, dedication and fear that the nuclear nightmare has inspired in millions of people"[16] so as to create an awareness that universal capitalism "is the *only* solution broad enough to heal our split society and promote ideological accord with the Soviets."[17]

But in making his points Speiser falls into the same ideological trap that has snared all of the pioneers of universal capitalism—the same ideological trap that for 25 years has prevented the Kelso theory from achieving a breakthrough to popular awareness.

The trap in question consists of believing that unconventional ideas can be successfully promoted in conventional terms. The pioneers of universal capitalism know they have a revolutionary concept by the tail. Indeed, they are highly excited by the world-shaking import of its tenets. But even though they are aware they are helping to blueprint the foundations of a *revolutionary new era* in human relationships, they have attempted to interpret its import in traditional terms—in the vogue of the present era.

The current vogue is the interpretation of ideas in terms of the prevailing left/right concept of social and political relationships. This dualistic concept represents the accepted frame of reference within which all the warring factions of the current world political scene agree to do battle. Communism, it is agreed, occupies the far "left" of the left/right spectrum, while capitalism occupies the far "right." All other social, political and economic points of view are thought to fall somewhere in between.

It is within the framework of this left/right way of thinking that Speiser presents his case. Universal capitalism, he believes, represents that singular *middle position* which alone can bridge the differences between leftist communism and traditional, rightist capitalism. "It brings together," he states, "the best elements of capitalism, socialism and Marxism."[18] But in attempting to make his case he speedily mires his argument in the ambiguities of left/right thought.

The left/right concept is an ambiguous concept because it depicts the systems of communism and traditional capitalism as absolute opposites when, in fact, they are closely related in their most basic aspects. Thus, Speiser finds himself both coming and going—talking about the two systems in flatly contradictory ways.

When Speiser describes the struggle between Communist Russia and capitalist America in traditional left/right terms, he sees a clash of irreconcilable ideologies: Thus are the battle lines drawn between the superpowers, each of which is committed to an economic system that is the antithesis of the other.[19]

But when he discusses the superpower relationships in terms of universal capitalism, he sees a much different economic situation. Instead of antithetical systems, he sees systems with similar internal problems. He sees the Soviet Union and the United States floundering in much the same basic economic dilemma:

> In the Soviet Union, as in the United States, 94 per cent of the population is denied access to their nation's wealth. Although technically the state owns the means of production, in practical terms the 6 per cent of Soviet citizens who are members of the Communist party control all of the nation's capital, creating a similar chasm between the haves and have-nots.
>
> ... It is a central irony of American-Soviet relations that the failings of both capitalism and communism have created similar internal problems—inequitable distribution of wealth, income and power.[20]

The similarity he depicts is that both the Soviet Union and the United States possess elitist economic systems—a similarity he discusses even more pointedly in yet another reference:

> Yes, that is what has brought the world to the brink of annihilation— two economic systems that are practically identical in the control of productive capital by an elite of about 5 per cent of the population! Percentage-wise, there aren't many more capitalists in America than there are Communist party members in Russia. Those members, the Soviet elite, get all the benefits of state-owned capital. The elite in America own the capital directly, but the effect is about the same. In neither country does the average citizen have a chance of gaining the main benefit of the economic system: capital ownership. And the supreme irony is that neither system works.[21]

What is going on here? Are the Soviet Union and the United States really the antithesis of one another? Or are they, in their elitist control of capital, practically identical?

Speiser is quite correct in stressing the elitist control of capital in both the Soviet Union and the United States. In so doing, he highlights one of the most telling—and most scandalous—features of Western cul-

ture. He highlights the fact that although the idea of democracy, the idea
of shared power, has been a dominant theme in Western culture for two
centuries, Western culture as a whole nevertheless continues to be highly elitist in character. Prattle as they may about their democratic intent,
all of the major Western powers—the Soviet Union and the United
States among them—adhere to rigidly elitist social and political practices.

Speiser is thus aware that societies everywhere in the world today
are being flim-flammed on the subject of democracy. He knows that
political democracy without economic democracy is a sham. Because
political power tends to follow economic power, he knows that the sharing of political power via the ballot box is not in itself an adequate test
of democracy. Not until economic power also is shared, through the
sharing of ownership of productive assets, will societies experience
democracy in its fullest sense, free of the arbitrary rule of privileged
economic elites.

Limitations of Left-Right Thinking

But what Speiser *does not* recognize is that the failure of most
people to recognize the importance of universal capitalism stems in
large part from the limitations of left/right thought itself—the system
of thought which is the hallmark of Western culture and which Speiser
himself continues to employ. He does not recognize that within the
left/right concept there is no alternative to the pervasive elitism that now
prevails. By pressing his case in terms of the left/right concept, he thereby insures that his arguments, like those of the other pioneers of universal capitalism, will go largely unheeded.

The inability of the left/right concept to depict the full process of
democratization—the inability of the left/right concept to reflect anything other than various elitist alternatives—is illustrated in Figure 1.
The illustration shows that within Western culture the process of
democratization, the sharing of power, has proceeded no further than
the alternatives of "rule by one" and "rule by a few." No provision for
"rule by many" (i.e., a sharing of economic power through widespread
ownership of productive capital) is offered under any of the major political alternatives. Instead, power is wielded by whatever elites happen to
gain control of a society's supply of productive capital.

On the left side of the left/right spectrum, control of capital is
wielded by *bureaucratic elites,* representing the power of centralized
governments and labor unions devoted to the principle of collective

Figure 1

ELITIST CHARACTER OF WESTERN CULTURE*

LEFT ←——— CENTER ———→ RIGHT		

Revolutionary Radicalism Radicalism	Liberalism Conservatism	Revolutionary Reactionism Reactionism
Communists Socialists (Russia) (England)	Democrats Republicans (USA) (USA)	Nationalists Fascists (Taiwan) (Germany)
Rule by One or a Few in a Collective Economy	**Rule by a Few in a Mixed Economy**	**Rule by a Few or One in a Private Economy**
No provision for assuring widespread ownership of productive capital. Instead, control of productive capital is concentrated in hands of *bureaucratic elites* (governmental and labor union) with control in highly authoritarian systems (Communist), narrowing to outright dictatorship.	No provision for assuring widespread ownership of productive capital. Instead, control of productive capital is concentrated in hands of *plutocratic elites,* such control, however, partially influenced, moderated or regulated by actions of *bureaucratic elites* (governmental, labor union).	No provision for assuring widespread ownership of productive capital. Instead, control of productive capital is concentrated in hands of *plutocratic elites* with control in the most highly authoritarian systems (Fascist), narrowing to outright dictatorship.

*Political movements identified in terms of representative ruling groups that have gained distinction on the world scene in the past half century.

economies.

On the right side of the left/right spectrum, control of capital is wielded by *plutocratic elites* made up of reactionaries and revolutionary reactionaries, representing the power of entrenched wealth devoted to the principle of private economies.

In the center of the left/right spectrum, control of capital is wielded by an uneasy balance of *plutocratic* and *bureaucratic* elites made up of representatives of entrenched wealth, working with liberals and conservatives in government and the labor unions in behalf of the principle of mixed economies.

The truth that fairly shouts at us from the diagram, therefore, is the fact that in all segments of the left/right spectrum, control of capital is covetously held in the hands of relatively small elites. Elitist control of capital is a given within the left/right concept. No provision exists within its confines for any other alternative.

More to the point, the idea of universal capitalism can find no logical footing within the context of the left/right concept.

Those on the left—those who believe in collective ownership of capital under the control of bureaucratic elites—dismiss the idea of universal capitalism as a "rightist" trick, a mere ruse for reinstating traditional capitalism and the principle of unfettered private economies.

Those on the right—those who believe in private ownership of capital under the control of plutocratic elites—dismiss the idea of universal capitalism as a "leftist" trick, a mere ruse for introducing communism and collectivism on an unprecedented scale.

Those in the center—those who believe in a balance between the forces of bureaucratic elites on the one hand and plutocratic elites on the other—dismiss the idea of universal capitalism as simply confusing and unsettling. In their view universal capitalism could conceivably lead to excesses of either the left or right. Its possibilities are therefore discounted accordingly.

In short, no one wholly immersed in the left/right way of thinking is listening.

Therefore, what the pioneers of universal capitalism must come to realize is that the prospects for economic democracy do not lie *within* the left/right concept, but in *transcending* that concept. They must come to realize that their insights into the workings of true economic democracy can be understood and appreciated only in terms of a larger and more comprehensive frame of reference which can encompass the process of democratization in its entirety, not just in part.

In bits and pieces such a new frame of reference is gradually emerging. It is emerging as part of the growing awareness of the importance of "process" as the most vital key to the understanding of every kind of human relationship, political or economic. In this case the process at issue is the process of democratization.

The Process of Psychological Maturation

The process of democratization is but one aspect of the overall process of *psychological maturation* which affects people both as individuals and as societies. Thanks to the process of psychological maturation, individuals can grow up, psychologically speaking, to become responsible adult human beings. And thanks to that same process of maturation, the aggregates of individuals we call societies also can grow up to become responsible democratic members of the world community. The maturation process for societies is not identical to that of individuals, but the two are closely related and their dynamics must be the focus of any meaningful system of social and political relationships.

In contrast, the left/right concept of social and political relationships attempts no such depiction. By its very nature, the left/right concept is more of an "equilibrium" concept than a "process" concept. Keyed to two violently opposing extremes, the left/right concept is used primarily to show how change can be kept to a minimum by a skillful balancing of forces. It is thus used more often to enhance and protect a prevailing status quo than to facilitate change toward any given end.

The process of social maturation, however, is decidedly goal-oriented. It is not used to enhance and protect the status quo so much as it is used to encourage the process of change, development and transformation that leads to a psychologically mature society.

The process of psychological maturation is essentially *cyclical* in nature. This, of course, is in contrast to the left/right concept which is linear. Because the left/right concept is limited to linear relationships only, the reason for its inability to reflect the process of psychological maturation becomes immediately apparent. A cyclical process can be effectively conceptualized only in terms of a cyclical image. It follows, then, that Western culture as a whole may never learn what is impeding its psychological development until it is able to conceptualize that development in cyclical terms.

Because we become individuals before we become members of a society, it may be helpful first to examine the process as it applies to individuals before moving on to social applications. The cyclical character of the maturation process is shown in Figure 2. Here we see that the

Figure 2

CYCLICAL THREE-STAGE PROCESS OF MATURATION

Maturity

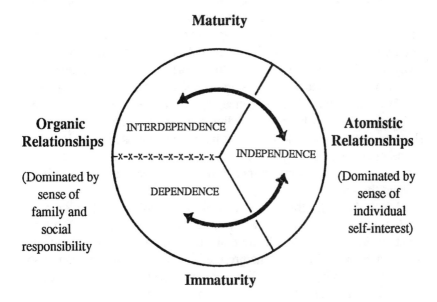

Immaturity

The maturation process involves three stages as shown above: "dependence," "independence" and "interdependence," with the middle step serving as the transition stage between immaturity and maturity. For immature individuals, the thrust of development moves away from dependence upon parental care and toward an independent existence dominated by a sense of self-interest. For mature individuals, the thrust of development serves to complete the cycle. It moves away from atomistic relationships of self-interest toward an interdependent, organic existence dominated by a sense of family and social responsibility.

The arrow are double-ended to show that the process, under certain circumstances, is reversible. The line of "X-X-X" indicates the natural limits to the process in either direction.

process occurs in three major stages—dependence, independence and interdependence—with the movement of development proceeding in a cyclical fashion so that the first and third stages become adjacent in proximity, sharing a common *organic* relationship.

The organic relationship that develops is between *dependent* infants on the one hand and *interdependent* parents on the other. Parents and infants share a very close organic relationship for a brief period in which the infant is almost totally dependent on the parents for assistance. But the process of maturation breaks up this close organic tie. The infant gradually acquires powers of its own, and as it does so, steadily moves away from the organic relationship toward a second, *independent* status in which the individual becomes preoccupied with its own self interest.

Once achieving independence, however, the normal course of maturation changes direction, heading back toward an organic relationship once again. Now, however, the individual begins to think in terms of the interests of others, marries, and enters into the third stage of *interdependence,* assuming responsibilities for the welfare of others beyond the self.

Much the same three-stage process of sociological development holds true for societies, as does the process of psychological development for individuals. It follows that the more mature the individuals within a society, the more mature the society itself will be. But also societies, as aggregates of individuals, have collective experiences in their own right. Indeed, they may have collective experiences continuing long beyond the lifespans of the individuals within the society—often for generations on end.

As with immature individuals, immature societies find themselves *dependent* on parental-type authority figures for guidance. Immature societies need such authoritative guidance to help them cope with the complexities of the modern world. And just as parental guidance on the family level is issued ostensibly in keeping with a sense of family responsibility, so parental guidance at the social level also is issued, ostensibly, in keeping with a sense of social responsibility.

In contrast, independent societies, like independent individuals, find themselves to have matured beyond the need for parental-type guidance and to have been able to institute self-governing practices of their own initiative and choosing. Having left the restraints of parental-type authority behind, independent societies, like independent individuals, at first tend to regard the exercise of social responsibility as repressive and to glory almost exclusively in the pursuit of self-interest.

Should independent societies and independent individuals fail to mature further and persist in a preoccupation with their own self-interest, they will become cases of *arrested psychological development*. They will continue to seek their own immediate gain without any regard for the needs of others, and consider it as a waste of time to worry about the legacy that might be left for future generations.

But if their psychological development is not arrested, if they continue to mature psychologically, independent societies and individuals alike will tend to experience a change of values. Their imagination will begin to expand so as to include an appreciation for the wants and needs of others. As this happens, their trajectory of development begins to change course. Instead of fleeing social responsibility and pursuing self- interest, they will move to complete the cycle, abandoning an exclusive preoccupation with self-interest in favor of a new, interdependent approach to social responsibility.

Such a new approach to social responsibility involves a decided shift in roles. The society or individual that earlier was the *recipient* of social responsibility exercised by a parental authority figure will now seek to assume a parental role in its own right and become the *bestower* of social responsibility on behalf of others.

What we are saying here is that both societies and individuals experience the second, independent stage of psychological maturation as a transition stage. A shift in roles must occur if the process of psychological maturation is to follow a normal course of development. And that course of development, as illustrated in above Figure 2, involves a change in direction, a "completing of the cycle," so that instead of fleeing organic relationships, a society or individual attempts to become involved in organic relationships once again.

The question of whether a society as a whole will actually develop in maturity to the point of completing the cycle and developing a strong sense of interdependence depends ultimately upon the proportion of mature individuals within the society and upon their understanding of the maturation process:

- as long as the models of maturity within a given society are perceived to be those who give unswerving and unquestioning obedience to a paternal dictatorship, that society will remain in the initial stage of sociological *dependence*.

- as long as the models of maturity within a given society are perceived to be the independent and wealthy few, who for one reason or another appear to have been the most successful in "standing on their own," that society will remain in the second stage of sociological *independence*.

- not until a significant number of individuals arise within a society to serve as models of a higher, *interdependent* level of maturity, will the society as a whole be inspired to negotiate the difficult cyclical change in thinking which calls for a serious and active awareness and concern for the wants and needs of the human species as a whole.

Such a cyclical change in thinking requires a strong development of selfhood. It requires a selfhood so strong and secure that it can become concerned with the welfare of others without feeling its own security threatened. Mature individuals and societies must necessarily have broad shoulders—capable of carrying the burden of concern, not only for the cares of the self but for the wants and needs of others, wherever they may be.

The Barrier of Social Conditioning

In noting the above, however, we are suddenly struck by the significance of a major difference between the psychological development of individuals and societies. It is not a difference in innate potential for psychological development. It is a difference in social "conditioning." Individuals, generally speaking, are socially conditioned to complete the maturation cycle, at least to some degree. Modern societies are not.

That is to say, individuals for the most part may not have had a cyclical image as such in their minds to condition their thinking and behavior with respect to the maturation process. But this lack has been offset by the fact that individuals in most cases have had immediate role models to follow (usually parents), whose examples have provided a vivid awareness of what completing the maturation cycle and evolving to the third stage of psychological *interdependence* is all about.

But this kind of conditioning has not prevailed for societies. Modern societies have had neither role models nor a realistic image of the maturation process to condition their development toward psychological maturity. As a result, the conditioning of most modern societies has been such as to suspend them, almost indefinitely, in a state of arrested psychological growth!

Thus, in terms of present-day political groupings, Communist societies fall rather clearly into the category of those arrested at the level of psychological and sociological *dependence*. All Communist societies are dependent upon authoritarian, parental-type governments for their decision making. And although segments of all Communist societies may well have matured beyond the need for such parental-type guidance, the societies as a whole are unable to institute self-governing practices, inasmuch as the Communist systems of which they are a part require that they remain in perpetuity as docile, dependent recipients of the parental guidance which their leadership forcibly thrusts upon them.

Capitalist societies, on the other hand, fall just as clearly into the category of those arrested at the level of psychological and sociological *independence*. They have matured beyond the need for parental-type guidance; they have instituted self-governing practices of their own choosing, but they have trouble in completing the maturational cycle. Despite many attempts and some partial successes in moving toward a more mature, *interdependent* world order, they have been unable to do so on a sustained and enduring basis. They continue, by and large, to exhibit the dominant trait of independent societies: they tend to glory in the pursuit of narrow self-interest.

The difficulty lies in the fact that Western culture as a whole has been suffering from a case of arrested sociological development. Its development has been arrested because its thinking has been shackled by the limitations of left/right thought. As shown in Figure 3, left/right thought can envision no significant alternative to the grim struggle now ensuing between leftist elites and rightist elites. It is at this level of development, the level of *leftist elites versus rightist elites,* that the maturational advance of Western culture has been arrested. And it is at this level that Western culture will remain as long as its thinking is dominated by the left/right dualism.

But it is this state of arrested development that is now subject to change. An entirely new system of thinking is bursting through into the realm of Western consciousness, a system that recognizes the pervasiveness of *process* as a basic reality of existence. It is a concept able to depict that particular process of *sociological maturation* by which humankind can indeed now transcend the current left/right stalemate and actually pursue its development toward a truly interdependent world community.

No small part of this breakthrough will consist of the fact that the pioneers of universal capitalism have already worked out many of the economic details by which a new era of sociological interdependence can be implemented. In championing the principle of universal capitalism, Louis Kelso, Norman Kurland, Patricia Hetter, Stuart Speiser and others already are helping to chart the way in which a more sociologically mature world community can be structured. Their efforts

Figure 3

LIMITATIONS OF THE LEFT/RIGHT DUALISM

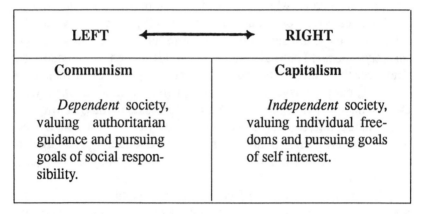

A dualistic concept is limited to the consideration of but two basic alternatives or extremes. Within the prevailing left/right concept of social and political relationships as it is used in the world today, the two extremes are communism on the "left" and capitalism on the "right" as shown above.

But precisely because it is limited to the linear portrayal of only two basic alternatives, the dualism is incapable of portraying more complex, non-linear relationships, such as are involved in the three-stage process of sociological maturation.

Because of its limitations, the left/right concept distorts and misrepresents the relationship of communism to capitalism. The two alternatives are not mutually exclusive extremes as pictured. Instead, they represent but the first two stages of *dependence* and *independence* in the three-stage, non-linear process of sociological maturation.

If the world community is thus to break out of the current left/right political stalemate and the nuclear standoff it entails—if it is to evolve to the third and more mature stage of sociological *interdependence*—it must first break out of its preoccupation with the left/right concept itself.

in behalf of more equitable and just economic systems mark them as leadership models of the higher, interdependent level of maturity required of the era ahead.

A Higher Level of Societal Maturity

An attempt to diagram the process of sociological maturation as it applies to societies is set forth in Figure 4. "Rule by one" is seen to be the characteristic social order for sociologically *dependent* societies, communism representing the most common such form. "Rule by a few" is seen to be the characteristic social order for sociologically *independent* societies, capitalism representing the most common of these. And "rule by many" is seen to be the characteristic social order for sociologically *interdependent* societies, the term "universalism" being suggested here as perhaps appropriate for such a new order, no major examples of which currently exist.

No major modern society has yet achieved the level of universalism in any meaningful sense, inasmuch as none has yet had the courage to abandon elitist control of productive capital. None has yet developed a systematic means of insuring widespread ownership of capital among their citizens at large. And that, of course, is what the principle of universal capitalism is all about.

How, then, would universalism differ from the liberalisms and socialisms now attempting to introduce a sense of social responsibility into national and world affairs?

Universalism would differ in that the sense of social responsibility would not be exercised in the form of setting up new elites to act on behalf of the disadvantaged. That is to say, new bureaucratic elites would not be established in government or labor unions to combat the alleged rapaciousness of plutocratic elites in private business. Instead, universalism would share power so broadly, so universally—both politically and economically—that privileged elites as such would no longer be dominant as before. Elitism of some type must inevitably prevail in all mature societies to some degree, but it makes a great deal of difference whether that elitism is based on merit or special privilege as it has so often been heretofore. Universalism will insure that all citizens have reasonably equal opportunity to become "elites of merit." Then, and only then, will any society achieve the third level of societal maturation—the level of sociological interdependence.

Much needs to be done in the way of spelling out the implications of the maturation process before it will become acceptable to those

Figure 4

THREE STAGES OF SOCIAL MATURATION

Fluid Relationships

(Providing for democratic opportunity)

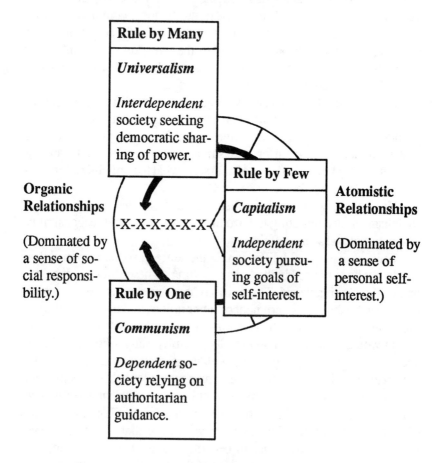

Hierarchical Relationships

(Providing for rigid governmental structures)

steeped in the old, dualistic way of thinking. But one implication of the image of that process already is clear, and that implication should go far toward gaining the acceptance of many. It is the implication that the cyclical image of the maturation process has the potential of wiping away the basis of much of the fear and despair that increasingly has gripped the world community during the past two centuries.

This fear and despair have been derived from the old left/right dualism. It is the belief that the world is trapped between two implacable and irreconcilable political "extremes." These extremities are today locked in such bitter ideological rivalry as to leave the rival camps no alternative but to threaten one another (and the world at large) with ever more destructive nuclear weapons, positioned for an even shorter delivery time.

Our new image resolves such foreboding fears with the realization that the belief in two such irreconcilable political extremes does not derive from any demonstrable characteristic of human development as such, but solely from the structure and limitations of the left/right way of thinking.

It is the left/right concept, not the process of human development, that is limited to two extremes. It is the left/right concept, not the human condition, that is bereft of alternatives.

All that is needed to escape this left/right dilemma is to abandon the left/right concept itself. To do so, we have only to shift gears in our thinking. Instead of thinking dualistically, we have only to think in terms of process. And when we think in terms of process, we see ourselves embarked on a new and challenging adventure.

The new adventure, as revealed in the cyclical process of maturation, is the adventure of "growing up" sociologically. It is the adventure of transcending the current left/right impasse through the development of a more mature, interdependent world community.

Editor's Comments

Like Wisman, Krough attacks the presumption that we can make peace in the world through creating ideological compatibility. In Krough's terms if we were to attain ideological convergence, it would not change the fact that the US is centered in the independence stage of maturation, while the USSR struggles to liberate itself from the dependence stage. What Krough does not explore is the role ideology plays in arresting development. If ideology, as Wisman believes, serves to explain reality and legitimize existing institutions, it thereby creates an acquiescent people and retards change.

A new ideology centered around a more "interdependent" view of reality may very well raise the general level of consciousness concerning existing societal institutions and motivate people to change them. Therefore, achieving ideological convergence may precipitate a more rapid advancement of a culture to the next highest stage—that is, if the newly formed ideology is truly compatible with the next higher stage. Krough does hint that the new ideology would embrace the concept of economic democracy as well as a new concept of societal reality—his social maturation process. Getting from here to there is a crucial question, and one he does not really address.

He does note that a prerequisite for emergence of an interdependent society is that a critical mass of individuals within society must have attained that level within themselves. This seems to imply that brute institutional change on the macro level will not achieve the desired evolution. We may deduce from this that Krough may have objection to a congressionally legislated USOP. In this view true societal advancement is likely to come from the individual, not the state. Christopher Budd's contest paper, "The Metamorphosis of Capitalism," addresses this very point.

Contribution by Christopher Budd

We have spoken of "economic freedom" (economic democracy). By it we mean something quite specific, namely, that the individual, on the one hand, has free access to capital and, on the other, that he not only looks after his own just interests in the use he makes of it, but that he consciously acts to benefit his fellow-man. A rich man who has stolen his wealth, for example, or one who has acquired it by cheating or underpaying workers, does not enjoy economic freedom. Nor, one could say, does the man who squanders it only on himself. And there is not much economic freedom if one's wealth has to be surrounded by security devices and the like, or if it hollows out the soul.

While something specific is meant by it, economic freedom is not readily defined. One could perhaps suggest that it obtains where no one feels that his gains, or those of another, have been ill-gotten. It does not mean that everyone will be hugely rich, which not only would deny the immense variety of human life but would contemplate an inconceivable economic condition. There will, however, be no feeling of inequity involved.

Whereas one cannot, with safety, *prescribe* what equitable conditions consist of, one can fairly readily *describe* conditions that are inequitable. Because the ideas of economic freedom and equitableness have an inner significance in the first place, they can then be translated into outer circumstances. But it is to be doubted that one can force them into being by manipulating outer conditions. Admittedly, this is to express the sociological view that real outer change derives from prior inner development, an approach to sociology of change that some would regard as naive.

Not so this writer. After all, the notion that American capitalism can be modified without adopting socialism or giving up treasured freedoms presupposes peaceful development. It presumes that within American capitalism as it stands, there are elements that can be modified and given new dimensions without involving major or violent external upheavals—and above all without these changes making American capitalism appear weak, let alone actually becoming so. It presupposes, too, that within those who practice American capitalism, there is a nascent development in this direction. In the end social and economic life results from what people will, and no plan for change will achieve very much if it does not describe something that can be humanly achieved.

Suffice it to say that the foregoing considerations imply a metamorphosis of capitalism. By metamorphosis we mean an external change that derives from inner changes so that outer things fall away by a process of being sloughed off, not stripped away from outside. From this point of view, the inequitable conditions that surround us today, along with the many social and political problems that characterize contemporary social life, do not signal that these things should change and need to be forced to do so from outside, but that they are already changing. What is lacking, however, is a clear understanding of these circumstances.

In a word, the conditions we see around us are as much due to the outmoded terms of reference we use to describe them, as they are to their actual existence. This is not to apologize for or to refuse to see the reality of life. But it is to argue that the idea of a metamorphosis of capitalism leads to a quite different assessment of the origin and nature of the world's problems and of the prospects for their resolution.[22]

In this passage Budd seems to affirm Krough's ideas of economic democracy, social maturation and the inappropriateness of current ideological thinking. Budd also reinforces Krough's argument that the direction of causation flows from individuals to social institutions. Both of these essayists lend support to Wisman's idea of promoting worker self-management as well as Rabow and Sappington's grassroots approach. Small-scale, community-based employee-owned enterprises might create the needed "demonstration effect"—the necessary role models to nudge along the consciousness-raising process in America. Once the critical mass of individuals have attained the interdependence mentality, a USOP might well be the next logical step in the social maturation process.

One other essayist also concluded that the left-right mode of thinking was excessively limiting in a dynamic world and that a new way of viewing society was in order. The view developed by Florian Zalewski's essay contest paper, "Property and Peace: Exploring the Foundations of Widespread Capital Ownership," was strikingly similar in this respect to Kenneth Krough's. The following excerpt illustrates the character of Zalewski's model of societal stages.

Contribution by Florian Zalewski

There are three possible types of national economic organization. These can be termed "collectivist," "individualist" and "solidarist." The common thread in all of them, of course, is that they reflect the combined impact of a very large number of individual actions.

The first type—a collectivist economy—is one in which most major economic decisions are centrally made. It is based on the assumption that an economy based on centralized decision-making is the best way to achieve satisfaction of a wide range of individual needs. The major consequence of this approach to human economic organization is that very often it degenerates into the wholesale use of force and terror to achieve its objectives.

In any society individuals have goals or needs independent of social or collective plans. Those in authority often have a difficult time accepting the idea that others have goals different than theirs. This divergence of goals and the failure to achieve them leads the political community to frustration. This frustration finds its outlet in the use of force to attain the economic goals determined by the leadership. Extreme frustration leads to violent resistance, which impels those in authority to respond with correspondingly violent repression of any who stand in the way. So the ideal of a better life for all actually results in the incarceration or even death of many.

A more sullen type of resistance leads to a decline in productivity as more people refuse to give their full cooperation to the economic process, frustrating achievement of the goals of centralized collective endeavors.

A national economy characterized by large numbers of powerful people, who concentrate on their own economic welfare and gains and pay little or no attention to the social consequences of their economic actions, is an "individualist" economy. Most Western capitalist societies reflect more or less an individualist economic orientation. A major consequence of this orientation is the accumulation of huge amounts of capital under the control of small numbers of owners or trustees. This effectively shuts out the vast majority of workers from a share in the ownership of the capital which their labor has generated. It makes them totally dependent on their labor for their economic welfare. It leaves them economically exposed during times of sickness, unemployment and old age. It sets the stage for the welfare system and the collectivist economy that so often flows from this sense of economic insecurity.

Individualist economic behavior sees only the individual's economic welfare and forgets that individual welfare depends on cooperative action with others and the decisions, for good or ill, made by others. The individualist tends to overlook the fact that his own self-interest is often bound up with a reasonable concern for the interests of those with whom he or she relates.

On the community or national scale, when large numbers of people feel that their economic interests are not being given sufficient attention, they tend to support the political expropriation of the wealth of the most successful, either directly through nationalization or indirectly through higher and higher taxes.

This expropriation of wealth raises the level of hostility between social classes. Higher levels of hostility between classes mean less cooperation and correspondingly slower economic progress. On the international level, such expropriation provides the basis for the hostility that has developed over the last 60 years between America and the Soviet Union.

At its inception the Soviet Union followed a policy of expropriation against all the wealthier classes. American leadership, seeing this and feeling more threatened as the Soviet Union extended its hegemony over more nations, developed a great mistrust of this expansionism and its implications for the capital owning classes. That mistrust expressed itself in the development of a large military and nuclear capability to contain Soviet expansion. The Soviets responded in kind and developed their own nuclear capability. This capability for mutual destruction began in human action aimed at improving the lot of the masses. It can only be eliminated or reduced by human action seen as holding out hope for a better life for the many.

The third possible type of national economic organization is called "solidarist" for several reasons. The first is that it attempts to coordinate and harmonize the social and personal aspects of humanity. It does not see these two as opposites but parts of a whole. It realizes that the individual needs the social in order to fully develop himself. The social exists for the personal. But the social or the collective must not swallow the individual. There needs to be a balance.

The solidarist, noting that human needs and interests are so varied, realizes that they can be satisfied only through organizations that mediate between the individual and the collectivity. This is so because the individual has needs that he or she cannot fulfill by relying on his or her own resources.

Since many of these needs are specific only to small groups of individuals it makes little sense to subject them to the detailed control of the national government. There are also wide variations in natural resources, land fertility, climate and other phenomena which shape the economic life of local communities and regions, not to mention human talents and desires in different communities. Hence the solidarist prefers to see resources and capital ownership, and economic decision-making widely distributed.

Realizing that human needs are ongoing and that many sophisticated economic processes take a long time to develop to their fullest potential, the solidarist favors long-term secure ownership rights. At the same time the solidarist realizes the changeability of economic conditions. Therefore, he favors the freedom to buy and sell capital and labor with a minimum of government interference.[23]

So the idea of ideological convergence takes on new form. Speiser's contention is that ideological change which enhances economic democracy creates a consequential movement toward ideological compatibility with Marxism. This in turn would reduce the ideological rhetoric, enhance mutual trust and bring the US and the USSR to the bargaining table of peace in good faith. Wisman agrees with the first part of Speiser's analysis, yet emphatically rejects the second part. Wisman's analysis concludes that ideology disguises the true source of friction and that the best way to encourage peace is to demonstrate to the Soviets that we mean them no harm and to modify existing capitalist institutions to enhance macroeconomic stability. That his proposed program achieves ideological convergence is secondary to it achieving other objectives. If ideological convergence happens, and hostilities continue, what then explains reality? Krough's contribution begins to fill this void. His analysis suggests that there are alternative means for interpreting and understanding societies. He also sheds light on the keys to societal evolution which can be used in framing proposals for institutional change. The brief excerpts from Budd and Zalewski add different tints to that light.

This brings us full circle back to Marx and his perception of human behavior and societal institutions. While Krough refrains from calling his paradigm a new ideology, he does stress process as fundamental to understanding society. In doing so he resurrects the historical dialectic Marx was so fond of. In the dialetical context capitalism and communism become thesis and antithesis. The resolution of the two opposing ideologies becomes the synthesis. This synthesis, this new ideology, would transcend the rhetoric of the old ideologies, forming a new set of criteria upon which to evaluate society. Krough's analysis does in fact begin to do all these things.

But whereas Marx believed that existing societal relations mold human consciousness, Krough suggests that there is also an important causal flow from individuals to institutions. Marx's belief that there is a single direction of causation led him to the conclusion that to change consciousness in general, social institutions must be forcibly changed through revolution. Krough's argument that a natural maturation process is unfolding within the setting of reciprocal influence between individuals and social institutions suggests the possibility of a peaceful transition to a higher state of mass consciousness.

IV

POWER, IDEOLOGY AND CULTURE

Editor's Introduction

To comprehend fully the impact ideological convergence would have on Soviet-American relations, we need a better grasp of the historical interaction between these two nations and their respective power structures. Only then can we understand the reasons for the nuclear nightmare in which we live and the prospects for stopping the arms race.

Robert Whealey's essay, "How to Get Along with the Soviet Union," contains a wealth of information on American foreign policy and the underlying motivations of the Soviet Union. Excerpts from his paper provide a new perspective from which to judge the effort to create ideological compatibility. (Numbers within parentheses refer to pages in Stuart M. Speiser's *How to End the Nuclear Nightmare* [Croton-on-Hudson, NY: North River Press, 1984].)

Contribution by Robert Whealey

A peaceful foreign policy must be based on an understanding of geography. This was the strength of two of the most successful diplomats America has ever produced, namely, John Quincy Adams and Henry Kissinger. Both had extensive experience with Europe, so neither was caught in a traditionally American provincial mindset, stemming partly from insufficient training in geography. The isolated security of the US from 1783 to the beginning of World

War II also contributed to this provincialism. Americans during this era felt no need for and generally opposed a large military establishment. This was in sharp contrast to other great powers more subject to invasion—like Russia. However, since the Second World War and the coming of the air age, a pro-military attitude has developed, under which Americans have imitated the worst features of their former enemies, the Germans and the Japanese. Americans thus seem to have learned the wrong lessons from World War II.

The Soviet menace, real though it is, has been greatly exaggerated and distorted by the mass media and corporate interests, and by politicians in Congress, the Pentagon and the White House. Much of the written history covering Soviet-American relations since 1945 tells us more about American images of Soviet policy than about Russian diplomacy itself. The Soviets do, as Winston Churchill put it in 1946, exhibit "expansionist tendencies," but the Soviet Union remains the number two power, while the US is number one—if one measures power economically, politically, ideologically and militarily. The USSR, however, does have sufficient power to say "no" to the US.

The Soviet Union is composed of some 270 million human beings who have very different geographic and economic interests from the inhabitants of the United States. The earlier histories of the two giant nations, going back 200 years, have been so different ideologically that it has been very difficult for the two peoples to understand one another. Yet historical fate since 1945 has cast the two into the same lifeboat.

Since 1945 the terminology of anti-communism,[1] used by the Pentagon, the State Department, eight presidents and the mass media, has had patriotic populist support. Most American leaders have become captives of their own propaganda. The American military blunders in Korea, Cuba, Indochina and Central America stem from a failure by Washington to define, at least within the bureaucracy, its own interests clearly. The blunders also stem from labeling various social revolutions as "aggression" and blaming the Soviet Union for indigenous social conflicts throughout the Third World. The Soviet Union has certainly been guilty of attempting to exploit these crises, but the American accusations against the Soviets have had the tail wagging the dog. Limited Soviet encouragement of "anti-imperialists" on a global scale was remade in Washington into

"Soviet aggressors" and "Soviet puppets," which called for further development of indiscriminate nuclear weapons on the part of the military.

But these anti-Soviet "patriots" fail to ask themselves what they want from Moscow in concrete terms. Do they want the Soviet Union to dismantle its ICBM's? Do they want the USSR to give up its base in Cuba? Do they want the USSR to recognize the Polish trade union, Solidarity? Do they want to break up the USSR? If they want to achieve any of these aims, what specifically are they willing to pay?

The anti-Communist Americans have intimidated liberals for 60 years by trying to link the crimes of Lenin and the quite different crimes of Stalin backward in time to Marx, and during the last five or six years forward to Daniel Ortega of Nicaragua. The fact that the provincial Marxists have exploited blunders by the State Department in the social and economic struggles of under-developed countries cannot be blamed on Moscow. The real threats the Soviets pose for Washington are its propaganda, regional police repression and possibly clandestine aid to revolutionaries, rather than the construction of military targets for which American nuclear stockpiles have much utility.

The Soviet Union produces few if any goods which threaten American economic interests; rather it is our allies, particularly Japan, which are our economic competitors. The USSR also poses little ideological threat, for Marxism has been on the decline, over-all, in the industrialized world since the Second World War (96, 106-107, 117-118, 182, 190-191).* Wherever Marxism has triumphed by taking over a sovereign state—in Russia, 1917; Yugoslavia, 1943-45; China, 1949; Cuba, 1959; in Vietnam in two stages 1954 and 1975; and maybe in Nicaragua, Mozambique and Angola—such Marxist governments have gained power as a result of national revolutionary wars against imperial or hegemonic powers. Moscow, at least since the founding of the Cominform in 1947, has concentrated on national liberation movements rather than the

---

* Since the mid-1970s, capitalism is also in deep crisis with abnormal inflation and unemployment.

proletarian revolution.

Even with the best of good will, it will still be difficult to get along with the USSR because of Russian paranoia stemming from invasions over ten centuries. But in the words of Henry L. Stimson, former Secretary of War and Secretary of State, spoken on 11 September 1945 when contemplating the big bomb and recommending sharing atomic secrets: "The only way you can make a man trustworthy is to trust him; and the surest way to make him untrustworthy is to distrust him and show your distrust."[2] The American leaders and people for the most part have ignored that advice at their own peril for the last 40 years.

The Pentagon, instead of thinking about strategy in geographical, economic and historical terms, seems to be racing to make its own weapons obsolete in the effort to perfect technology. Within a few years, American innovations in the technology of destruction, such as the atomic bomb and MIRV, have been imitated by the USSR. Any sane politician with any hope for the future of his own people would set limits on further nuclear endeavors by mutually verifiable treaties. It may be a flaw in the American national character that assumes that technological solutions can be substitutions for political and moral positions.[3]

In dealing with the USSR, one can agree with Speiser on the necessity for ideological disarmament. I also have no quarrel with his stock option plan, which seems utopian but rational. But before the capitalists who control America (101-102, 190-191)—a mere 6 per cent of the American population—are going to allow Congress to pass legislation to implement Speiser's stock plan, a long debate will ensue. My proposals, like Sagan's and Schell's, are only stopgap plans (three or four nuclear treaties) to give humanity some limited arms control. These modest proposals may give us time to work on future ideological disarmament, a much more difficult task. Historically, ideological change is more difficult to achieve than Speiser imagines. Capitalism as practiced today dominates American society. It would be politically easier to get Congress to conclude another arms treaty with the USSR than to get them to implement Speiser's SuperStock Plan, which would entail a redistribution of property. Some ideological modification of American attitudes toward the USSR and communism, might take place simultaneously along with negotiation of arms treaties, but the sweeping change of his SuperStock Plan cannot.

The Soviet power elite or the "New Class," different in form and in ideological justification, but similar to the social structure in America (10, 70, 101), is also a problem in the USSR. But Speiser has a tendency to play down the impact of this Soviet bureaucracy on global military and diplomatic history since 1917. He also ignores the geopolitical dimensions of American foreign policy. He takes "Marxism" and "capitalism" and the entire ideological dimension of life in both countries far too seriously. George Orwell does not appear in his bibliography. Marxism is indeed taken seriously by Soviet educational institutions, but is manipulated cynically by the Politburo for the sake of power ploys. Paradoxically, capitalists in America, because of excess fear, guilt and ignorance, also take Soviet Marxist indoctrination too seriously. Keeping the Russians loyal to "communism" justifies their own blind anti-Communist policies pursued for the past 60 years.

A study of Stalin's zig-zags in international politics from 1924 to 1953 would cause one to doubt the importance of Soviet ideology. Stalin's domestic policy proves the point even more so. Stalin killed more Communists than any other man in history. Marx and Stalin were both too complex as people to support any sweeping statement about ideological determinism. Speiser's perception of Karl Marx is adequate, of Stalin non-existent, but quoting anti-Soviet dogmatists like Alexander Solzhenitzyn, Robert Conquest, Thomas Larson and Reagan's journalist Patrick Buchanan (72-76) on Marxism is superficial if not dangerous. Paradoxically, at other places Speiser recognizes the ideological flexibility of Khrushchev and Brezhnev.

As Speiser advocates, capitalism should be reformed on the basis of the needs of the American people, but to require this as a precondition of disarmament is too hopeful (see especially 257) of the ability of good will to triumph over vested interests.[4]

To understand why the Soviets cannot be expected to lead in the quest for ideological disarmament, one must understand the nature of the power structure of Soviet society. The following essay by Paul Grenier[5] is a study in the cultures of the superpowers, with particular attention to the Soviet Union. His analysis adds depth to Kenneth Krough's more abstract discussion of plutocratic elites and introduces us to the small percentage of Russians who are members of the Com-

munist party. In the process Grenier adds substantiating evidence to Jon
Wisman's conclusion that ideological convergence will not yield the
immediate results Speiser predicts. On the other hand, he surmises that
we need to take steps toward creating an "idealist culture." Doing so,
he argues, will help us to transcend, *a la* Kenneth Krough, existing warlike propensities, forming the foundation for future peace.

The Common Task: Peace Through Convergence Toward Compatible Ideals
by Paul Grenier

The Nature of Society

A number of my disagreements with Stuart Speiser's essay result,
in all likelihood, from the different meanings I attach to the words
society and ideology. These words are, of course, used in many different
senses—not only by the public, but by social scientists as well. This
makes it all the more necessary for me to clarify carefully the sense in
which I am using them before proceeding further.

First of all, I will admit to sidestepping an important question: does
"society" have its own separate *being,* or is it just a word used for convenience to mean the sum of many people taken together? Much
depends on how one answers this question, yet it seems best to avoid
answering it directly if, by answering it indirectly, one can retain some
of the insights of both sociological realism (society exists) and
sociological nominalism ("society" is just a word; only individuals
exist). And it seems that this can be done if we follow the Russian
philosopher Semyon Frank's practice of recognizing that, in any case,
one can certainly think of society as a unified system in the *logical* (if
not ontological) sense that it represents a single *interactive* system of
"a group of people taken as a whole" with "a group of people taken as
a plurality of separate parts (i.e., as individual humans or sub-sets of
the whole)." By "interaction" we mean that the one influences the other.
In this sense the word society could be applied even to such an entity
as the "group consisting of all the people in the United States and the
Soviet Union." The various parts of these two countries (their military,
political, artistic and agricultural centers, for example) often have a tangible impact on the other side, and the nature of the overall relationship—i.e., the system as a whole—often has a tangible impact on the
separate parts of this "society."

One could say, then, that what distinguishes one type of society from another is the kind and the degree (or intensity) of integration binding that society together. The mere fact of interaction—of relation—by no means implies a harmony of interests between the separate parts of society. There is no need to convince anyone that the separate actors in society can be motivated by distinctly different interests. And yet, if this is so, what prevents society from *always* living in the Hobbesian chaos of *bellum omnium contra omnes,* the war of all against all? The central question, then, from both the general theoretical perspective as well as that of our current problematic—the question of eliminating war—is this: by what means does society stay unified?

The answer given by Frank (and, in only slightly varying forms, by other eminent pre-Soviet Russian scientists, such as Petrazhitsky and Sorokin) again seems attractive; and, indeed, both more elegant and also truer than the vulgar answer of Hobbes and the one-sided answer of Locke. It is as follows. Certain ideal forms—for example, the ideal of friendship, marriage, family; the ideal of Nation; legal and economic concepts and forms—may be accepted by the individuals in a society as an ideal norm which they must strive to conform to, or to attain, in their own behavior. To the extent that these ideal forms *in fact* motivate the will of the individuals in society, they become the force which binds society into a real, and not merely an ideal or logical unity.[6]

To avoid objections it is necessary immediately to add that, of course, these ideal forms come to motivate the individuals in any particular society in different ways, depending on the qualities and character of its leaders and citizens. It may be by *compulsion.* It may be by *contract*—mutual agreement based on convenience to both parties. The idea of a free market economy is supposedly based on this type of motivation (and if all members of society were property owners such might be the reality). And, finally, there is love (Sorokin uses the term "familistic unity"): a spiritually free accord based on an inner identity of purpose and ideals.

Implicit in this definition is the idea that society is a human, artificial phenomenon, rather than a purely natural one. People act as they do in society primarily because the society as a whole has objectified in its customary living law, as well as in its enforced positive law, certain ideas as to how one should behave. The individual in society has, therefore, only a relative freedom, but the social system as such is absolutely free to redefine itself, as individual and society interactively change one another in accordance with new ideals, intuitions and aesthetics. (This suggests that society need not remain the way it is. But such a rejection of "realism" implies no support for utopianism; we are also free to reject both in favor of what Frank would call "ideal-realism.")

It follows from the above that any given society has its own peculiar *ideology* in the sense of its own set of values, norms, beliefs and mean-ings. Besides differing in their ideological content, societies differ in the extent to which the various meanings are logically and aesthetical-ly integrated. Unrelated meanings, such as *Anna Karenina* and a beer commercial, form what Sorokin called a *congeries*. The beatitudes and a gothic cathedral form one example of both logical and aesthetic in-tegration.

To be sure, one's professed ideals and values may be one thing, while one's overt behavior expresses values of an entirely different sort. Nonetheless, Sorokin's investigation of European history has shown that there is definitely a correlation between a society's social values and its actual overt behavior. Human behavior is not a constant throughout history.[7] The assumption widely held today that "real" motivations are always based, ultimately, on material sensory values is more likely an expression of current cultural values than the result of careful historical analysis.

What Sorokin's research clearly and empirically demonstrates is that throughout European history, main systems of values have fluc-tuated, leading to the domination of now an ideational, now a sensate, now an idealistic (or mixed) cultural system. A *sensate* culture, such as probably reached its culmination in late 19th century European civiliza-tion (the "Age of Materialism," according to many historians), holds that true reality and value is sensory; that beyond the reality and value perceived by our sense organs there is nothing but illusion. Such a culture's scientific, philosophical, ethical and artistic systems are shaped by this premise.

Other cultures have held that the true reality and value is a super-sensory, super-rational, Absolute Being (God, the Tao, Brahma). They regard sensory reality and value as being either an illusion or the least important aspect of reality. In Sorokin's terminology such a cultural sys-tem is called *ideational.*

Finally, the *idealistic* cultural system assumes that the true reality and value includes sensory, rational, and super-sensory and super-rational elements. The ideational and idealistic systems have, in turn, their corresponding systems of philosophy, science, ethics, art, etc.

In acknowledging the existence of these cultural systems one need not deny the truth that society is also shaped, in part, by purely elemental forces: individuals can and do act aimlessly, irrationally or according to purely biological motives. Finally, it must be noted that few if any historical cultures have manifested a pure ideational, idealistic or sensate culture. Nonetheless, history clearly establishes that these super-systems have existed as clearly predominant systems of truth and culture in individual societies.

American and Soviet Culture and Ideology

Later we will repeat in somewhat more formal language that the essence of building peaceful relations between nations (and social groups generally) lies in promoting the integration of, and greater compatibility between, the ideological (in the above sense) principles animating the groups in question. This daunting task must be preceded by yet another: the analysis and description of the ideological culture of the nations concerned, a task that F.S.C. Northrop felt should be assigned to a discipline he christened "philosophical anthropology."

No adequately detailed fulfillment of this task can be undertaken here, although the rough outlines of a response may be sketched. Now, it is enough to live in the United States, and to have eyes to see and ears to hear, to know that *as a single integrated system,* no "American culture" as such exists. American culture forms an even more fragmented and eclectic congeries today than it did 40 years ago when Northrop attempted to summarize the basic traits of American culture (and other cultures, including Russian) in his *The Meeting of East and West.*[8] The ever-present American eclecticism does not prevent us, however, from making any useful generalizations about American culture because, inasmuch as the US still maintains some cohesiveness as a society, it must also retain some of those ideal forms without which such complex forms as the national economy and national legal system could not exist. It is true that neither of these systems retain their former prestige; indeed, both are in decay. But the absence of any living replacement for them, together with their (albeit senile) continued life, justifies my allowing the principles behind these main cultural systems to represent what is most characteristic for contemporary American culture as a whole.

The sources of these systems, fortunately, are well known. Adam Smith, an intimate friend of Hume, conceived of the modern economic notion that value is not inherent in the object (nature or nature transformed), although he did not yet totally fulfill the (Humean) sensate definition that value inheres only in the purely relative sense of the impressions of any one person at any given moment. It remained for the later economist, Jevons, to do that. These remarks alone suffice to demonstrate that the classical Western (and US) economic concepts are sensate.

American law traces directly to Locke without the intermediary of Hume. For Locke, man was a "mental substance." But this contentless container could not even conceive of anything unless it was first gained by sense impression. Still, in Locke's legal thought as well as in the founding fathers' legal documents—the Constitution and the Declaration of Independence—ideas from an earlier era of a positive good not known through the senses still linger. At the same time, "truth" becomes relative to the varying impressions of the generic (and hence "equal") mental substances: jurors, voters and so forth.

It is safe to say that with further development American law has allowed the remnants of pre-sensate law to fall away. The modern legal sociologist Edwin Schur states that Sorokin "nicely captures some of the quality of modern views of law" when he states that it is viewed by a sensate society as:

> . . . man-made, frequently, indeed, as a mere instrument for the subjugation and exploitation of one group by another. Its aim is exclusively utilitarian; the safety, security, happiness of either society at large or of the dominating faction which enacts and enforces sensate law. Its norms are relative, changeable and conditional. Nothing eternal or sacred is implied in such a system of law.[9]

American concepts of international law and politics have come to reject Locke only to embrace Hobbes. Hobbes' image of humans as physical particles randomly bumping in space gives theoretical justification to the crudest power politics in international behavior where, supposedly, the original "state of nature" still reigns. This view of international law as coercion increasingly corrupts the American concept of domestic law as well.

In two major institutions, then—law and economy—the sensate character of US ideology is apparent, although the adherence to even these principles is devoid of reverence. It should also be made explicit, without at this point dwelling on the subject, that there exist in the US idealistic and ideational systems, but these do not come close to defining the character of the society as a whole.

As to the Soviet Union, it is my thesis that its main official institutions, including but not limited to its systems of law (politics) and economy, also belong to the sensate cultural type. A more detailed look at this "official," more or less logically integrated system of Soviet society follows. It bears noting right away, however, that—as was the case with the United States—it would be wrong to speak of a single unified Soviet cultural system permeated by the same cultural meanings. We should not imagine that Soviet society divides cleanly into separate categories of meaning along the lines of official and non-official culture.

Not all officially permitted art and thought are sensate. Some are idealist and even ideational; icons, as at least one example of the latter, still hang in Soviet churches and museums. Nor is all—or even most—underground Soviet culture anti-sensate. Soviet drug and rock culture, for example, shares the hedonist meaning of its Western counterparts, with perhaps the same percentage of exceptions to the rule. Meanwhile, Soviet-educated classes can read the officially accepted novels of Chingiz Aitmatov, whose themes are increasingly openly religious. And they listen to the mildly spiritual, romantic poetry of the officially tolerated Bulat Okudzhava.

But we must focus on picking out the main themes in the symphony. If the mass of Soviet youth, despite the alternatives, listens to rock music in preference to the Russian classical composers, still more so does the mass of Soviet officialdom listen to the dictates of Lenin and Marx; no "alternatives," thus far, have been tolerated.

The Causes of War

The above discussion of ideology and society does not aim at comprehensiveness; it aims simply at providing the minimum of context necessary to make understandable our model of the causes and cures of war—with special reference to the US-Soviet dimension. This model, in essence identical to that of Sorokin's, claims only a rough validity. Yet, as is often the case with Sorokin's formulations, it is at least firmly grounded in logic and consistent with historical fact, even if somewhat rough and general.

Few attempts at a *generic* definition of war as such have succeeded in finding a causal model that applies *in all cases*. A truly generic definition will list conditions which must be present for war to take place. If conditions opposite to these are present, war cannot take place. Now, a generic model (such as we consider Sorokin's to be) is clearly more logically compelling, and more practically useful, than an explanatory model which works only a certain percentage of the time. An explanation of cholera which applies only once in a while would not be considered very valuable.

The Sorokin causal model flows logically from the very nature of society. That nature presupposes the presence of a system of basic values and behavioral norms which may come to motivate society's members in various ways.

The generic cause of conflict can best be understood if one first considers the generic cause of harmony within a given society:

> The main cause of internal social peace is the presence in the given society of a well-integrated system of basic values, with their corresponding norms practiced in overt conduct. (Every basic value has its set norms of conduct, with their "thou shalt" and "thou shalt not." Religious, ethico-juridical, scientific, economic, political, aesthetic values—each has its code of conduct.) The fundamental values of the various factions and members of the society must be essentially in harmony with this system and with one another. The values must be based on the principle of the Golden Rule and not on that of hatred.[10]

Next, one should expand the society or social system to the dimensions of the international and observe that a similar set of conditions cannot but lead to the same result:

> The main cause of international peace is the presence in each of the interacting societies of a well-integrated system of basic values and their norms, all of which are *compatible* with one another, practiced by societies involved, and based on the Golden Rule.

Finally, the generic cause of war can be defined by negation:

> In a given universe of societies or within a particular society, the probability of peace varies directly with the integration of the systems of basic values and their mutual compatibility. When their integration and harmoniousness decline, especially suddenly and sharply, the chances for international or civil war increase.

The truth of the statements regarding the causes of peace I take to be intuitively obvious. A modern person may, of course, think they are overstated. Do we not observe the absence of war without all of this? Well, yes, we do: the point, however, is that wherever such conditions are given (assuming no exogenous interference) there *must* be peace. The closer any society *approximates* these ideal conditions, the better the chances for peace.

In the case of the causes of war, one's first reaction may not be intuitive agreement. This appears paradoxical since it is merely the reverse of the conditions for peace. At any rate, the historical evidence with which Sorokin has tested this theory—although I find it convincing—is far too voluminous to list here.[11] Even historical evidence, though, can only "prove" something within a given philosophical conception of causality, and this, no doubt, is the central issue.

The Aristotelian framework on causality is useful here in that it suggests, through the concepts of "efficient cause" and "final cause," something resembling the two types of causality I wish to distinguish. Some wars appear to have been accidental, others the result of unstable mad men. World Wars I's "efficient" cause may have been accidental. But not all accidents lead to war, just as not all hands pushing pens lead to novels. The important cause of World War I was that the political (nationalist-imperialist) values and, to a lesser extent, economic values of the European states, having lost their ability to integrate the respective nations, became relativized as well as conducive to extreme competitiveness. Thus, these value systems tended naturally to develop toward war—if perhaps without conscious intent. (Historian Marc Raeff would argue that even the conscious intent was present: war was indeed wanted, simply not the war they got.)

The "efficient" cause of World War II may have been Hitler, but of mad men there have been plenty throughout history. Only rarely do they "cause" wars. The key "final" cause of World War II, however, was German society's super-nationalist ideology of hate and Aryan supremacy, a system of values incapable of integration with other societies, and hence a socio-cultural phenomenon which could hardly but develop toward war.

Yet as the Austrians found this system of values compatible with their own, they did not go to war with Germany (although they hardly avoided violence and conflict!). Poland although her military situation was equally hopeless, did go to war. Stalin, as we know, took a slice of Poland (not to mention absorbing a few other neighbors and concluding a friendship treaty with Hitler), although in doing so he allowed Hitler to secure his Western front before attacking the Soviet Union. What this implies about Stalin's system of values I leave to the reader's imagination.

Another reason "moderns" (mainly academic moderns) so often fail to appreciate the importance of Sorokin's formulations has, of course, to do with the sensate philosophy and science that still largely defines accepted wisdom. University social science, by and large, remains wed (although true love is absent) to an externalistic, natural, science type of methodology. Despite a few noteworthy exceptions, most talk of ideology in political science is of the "factor" school; ideology is one of several "factors" causing this or that. Such an approach is merely a means of keeping one's intellectual bases covered. As Sorokin pointed out, however, if everything is caused by a set of external factors, this leads to the logical absurdity of an infinite series of external factors each causing the previous factor. The definition of society and the causal model of war developed in this essay avoid *reductio ad absurdum* by properly giving to values and cultural meaning the role of the primary, *immanent* dynamic of social change.

From this perspective, Speiser's system is in many ways refreshingly free of academic prejudices. He assigns to ideology a primary role in international conflict, looks at US and Soviet society as single systems, and advocates removal of a source of ideological conflict as a step toward the avoidance of war. His conception of ideology, however, is too limited. He does not sufficiently investigate whether common values are internally compatible. To comprehend better the compatibility of US and Soviet values, it is necessary to take a closer look at the values of that class which has traditionally been considered identical with all that is official in the Soviet Union: the *nomenklatura*.

The *Nomenklatura* and Marxist Ideology

The *nomenklatura*, which according to Voslensky makes up about 1.5 per cent of the total population of the USSR, is the ruling elite of Soviet society. In what sense and to what extent is Marxist ideology a value for the *nomenklatura*?

Marxist ideology is not valued as a system of truth. Neither Marxist truth nor truth per se are a value for the *nomenklatura* because the materialist philosophy on which it is founded, when consistently applied, must end by considering philosophy (love of truth) to be a mere epiphenomenon of material-technological processes and political force—the "real" and "true" determinants of all social phenomena. Power is the basic value of the *nomenklatura*.

In essence, Marxism is of interest to the *nomenklatura* only to the extent that it actually serves the *nomenklatura's* basic value. The "useful" truths of Marxist doctrine provide useful political and legal ideas. In the political realm it helps provide the justification for absolute dictatorship, which can be based on the materialist doctrine of society itself. Since the "true" or "basic" reality is exclusively material, the basis of societal unity must also be material. (Certainly it cannot be "ideal" or "ideal-real," as we have suggested above.)

Hence, insistence on a real, material unity of "society" with "the Party," as if in a single organism. "The Russian Bolshevik . . . cannot help regarding all this talk about 'from above' *or* 'from below,' about the dictatorship of leaders *or* the dictatorship of the masses, etc., as ridiculous and childish nonsense, *something like discussing whether a man's left leg or right arm is of greater use for him.*"[12] This "sacred" unity amounts to denying the individual any freedom of movement, a phenomenon reflected in the following incident:

> . . . In June and July of 1982, Shatravka and Mishchenko, . . . acquainted workers with the document "An Appeal to the Governments and Publics of the USSR and USA." This document is of an anti-Soviet nature . . . . The document contains an appeal to create independent social groups in the USSR and the USA. This means creating a dialogue between the USSR and the USA. This means creating groups separate from the struggle for the salvation of humanity that the Party and the government leads . . .[13]

Marxism is also useful to the *nomenklatura* by providing a materialist system of law the ultimate authority of which lies in the superior force of the ruling class. Marxism likewise claims that it does not merely rule in the interests of the majority, but as well is virtually identical with the entire society, providing a complete moral justification for any behavior whatsoever. Since, then, the Party's interests form an absolute, organic and factual unity with the interests of the entire people. Individuals who differ with the Party in any way can easily be declared "insane" by the State for not being aware of reality or for having "reformist delusions." "Rehabilitation" of such "mentally ill" persons consists essentially in the infliction of pain and the use of force until the "patient realizes his unity" with the Party. In the case of the psychiatrist Anatoly Koryagin, who tried to protest this degradation of psychiatry, the effects of his "rehabilitation" may have already killed him.

Similar use of such crude materialist formulas lies at the foundation of other systems in the *nomenklatura* socio-cultural universe in philosophy, ethics and aesthetics. That all of this is a crude coarsening of Marxism is undeniable, but as Leszek Kolakowski pointed out in his magisterial study, ambiguities in Marx's thought make such interpretations possible, even inevitable, *when it is actually put into practice.*

Many aspects of Marx's thought are, of course, not useful to the *nomenklatura.* His ideas on democracy under socialism, his absolute condemnation of censorship and his entire book on Russia's secret diplomatic history are all censored from Marx's collected works. Actual ownership of the means of production is by the tiny—and also secret (its existence is denied)—*nomenklatura,* although by the same materialist magic they are also owned "by the entire people."

Is, as Speiser states, Marxism necessary to the Soviet government? Only to the extent, *and in the form that,* the *nomenklatura* finds useful for its own ends. As the ability of Marxist dogmas to motivate the general Soviet population decreases, the importance of unadorned national chauvinism as a replacement has tended to increase.

This last point, however, is not crucial. For the sake of argument, let us suppose that the *nomenklatura* continues to retain Marxist phraseology to support its absolute control of society. If it is really true that the Soviet governing elite does not seek "global conquest," as Speiser (along with others) would tend to believe, and if we can find a way to let the Soviets call us "Marxist," perhaps we can still live together in peace, albeit only if we offer them the opportunity to join us in a worldwide partnership.[14]

I disagree with this view for the following reason. Even if the *nomenklatura* does not consider "global domination" its "basic goal," the *nomenklatura's* need for removal of Western non-socialist systems runs deeper even than their also quite real desire for expanding their power bases. It is simply a necessity, *given the nature of the present values and norms of the nomenklatura, with their corresponding compulsory-antagonistic social and cultural institutions,* and given the *nomenklatura's perception that these values and norms conflict with those of their subjects in the Soviet Union and its dependencies.*

> The existence of the non-socialist world, in the eyes of the *nomenklatura*, serves as the source of a constantly fermenting internal discontent in the Soviet Union and other socialist countries. The combination, in Europe and North America, of a free, parliamentary system with an extraordinarily high, from the Soviet viewpoint, standard of living in these countries, exerts a strong magnetic pull on the populations of the socialist bloc. Since it is virtually impossible to leave the Soviet Union and go to the West, this magnetic pull becomes a source of irritation, dislike, and, in the end, hatred for the system of "real socialism." A particularly important role, in this respect, is played by Western Europe. And this is why [the *nomenklatura*] considers the question of Western Europe particularly urgent.[15]

Speiser has correctly pointed out that the pseudo-justice of communism exerts a certain pull on populations disaffected with their social system, especially in the Third World. He has, however, neglected to note that the real, if flawed, attractions of even "bourgeois" freedom, including some non-trivial freedoms and rights in the legal, religious, informational and other realms of socio-cultural existence in the West, are positive values for much of the *Soviet* population. That the *nomenklatura* believes this is true is proven by its strenuous efforts to isolate its population from the West, to distort and especially to restrict information from outside their control. In order to remove this threat to *nomenklatura* rule in its present form, it would be necessary for the West "to renounce its own freedom and well-being (*blagosostoyaniye*), to eliminate every advantage it has over real socialism."[16]

Thus, for all its attractions, the democratization of capital ownership in the United States is powerless to eliminate the source of ideological conflict with the Soviet Union. Even if the American concept of law had already degraded to the state of Soviet law—which I do not think it has—this would only make our two systems *more* incompatible. (Until our two nations adopt a truly compatible system of law, will not all international agreements according to "international law" be unworthy of the paper they are written on? I examine this problem in the next section of my essay.)

Despite all of the above, if we nonetheless proceeded to act on the assumption that we had achieved a *general* ideological reconciliation based on this partial—and, as we have seen, superficial and one-sided reconciliation—this could only lead to all sorts of untoward and undesired results. This is particularly true in the case where we formed a "worldwide partnership" within which we could jointly satisfy our "desire for power."[17] On the one hand, we could acquiesce in the denial to other nations—European and non-European, aligned with the US or non-aligned—by violent means (including subversion) of those fundamental rights that more than in our present system of semi-laissez-faire capitalism we *should* consider "non-negotiable." Such passive acquiescence would amount to a policy not only of extremely questionable moral worth. In the long run it would be self-defeating, inasmuch as we would eventually find the "global correlation of forces" so shifted against the US that defense of even those "fundamental values" would prove problematic.

Given the Soviet *nomenklatura's* present values we have no rational basis to assume they will cease efforts to eliminate alien systems manifesting values they fear. And so, if on the other hand, we choose a course consistent with "true" values, and continue to extend the promise of our support to other nations in order to deter Marxist subversion or outright invasion, we simply find the global balance of tensions to be more or less where it was prior to the reforms in the US economy. There is no question but that we should choose this second course. This means that a long-term strategy for overcoming the essence of the ideological conflict with the USSR and removing the global problem of war remains to be formulated. This is an enormous task. Nonetheless, taking

heart from Speiser's boldness in starting just such a project, I, too, will
have the audacity to continue it.

The Search for an Idealistic Culture

Rudolf Steiner once wrote somewhere that men who are too practical end up being not practical at all. (Apparently women were spared
this vice.) A practical person assumes that "self-interest" and the urge
to power are "natural." And yet, if one "remains neutral" about self-interest, one cannot hope to do away with war. At the same time, as
Solovyov has pointed out, "self-interest" comes in two varieties—
material and spiritual—and neither is more "natural" than the other.

The path of material self-interest is "natural for animals, just because animals do not decide anything, do not choose between this path
and any other, but passively follow the only one upon which they have
been placed by a will foreign to them. But when man *actively* decides
to follow the path of moral *passivity,* he is clearly guilty of falsehood
. . . and is obviously entering not upon the animal path, but upon that of
the two human paths which proves, in the end . . . to be the path of eter-
nal evil and death."[18]

In describing the causes of peace, Pitirim Sorokin found that the
basic values of the social system (whether a plurality of societies or a
single society) must be *compatible.* The fact that the basic values of a
society (or of societies) may be identical does not make the value system internally compatible, because there are values which are internally contradictory and morally inconsistent. This is why Sorokin further
stipulated that the basic values of a harmonious social system must be
based on "The Golden Rule" and "not on hate."

It is the reign of an unbalanced sensate culture in the USSR and the
United States that makes the two societies incompatible with one
another and internally divided within. To the extent that they are sensate, and therefore assign to the *material* primary importance, the values
of the two societies are not different but identical. Although the forms
are different, the inner principle is the same. This is particularly evident
in the realm of economics. Although many think of socialism as the
anti-thesis of capitalism in this respect, in reality the opposite is true.
Socialism is the extreme expression of capitalist bourgeois culture.

> Socialists and their apparent opponents—the plutocrats—uncon-
> sciously join hands on the most essential point. Plutocracy subjugates
> the masses of the people to its own selfish interests, disposes of them
> to its own advantage, for it regards them merely as labor, as producers

of material wealth. Socialism protests against such "exploiting," but its protest is superficial and is not based upon principles, since socialism itself in the long run regards man as *merely* (or in any case mainly and primarily) an economic agent—and if he is only that, there is no *inherent* reason why he should not be exploited.[19]

Anyone who reads through all of Voslensky's *Nomenklatura* (an English edition was published by Doubleday in 1984) will find that materialist socialism has indeed found that there is no reason not to exploit man; it uses Marxist theory so as to refine the exploitation even more scientifically.

It is not economic inequality that is the root of evil, but the subjugation of human beings to *matter*. "The human mind can and must liberate within itself energies greater than those within stones and metals, lest the material atomic giant, newly unleashed, turn on the world in mindless destruction."[20]

What should replace the sensate culture? An *idealistic* culture. It cannot be an ideational culture because the majority in any society at the present historical moment is not ready to abandon all material concerns in order to devote their lives to the search for God and Absolute Truth. To demand or to expect it would make society too unstable and dogmatic and lead to such war-like theocracies as Iran, which in turn leads to a violent reaction in favor of sensate culture.

The defects of sensate culture we have already seen. Only idealistic culture is sufficiently balanced to conform to the needs of historical society, and profound enough to help raise society above its lower concerns for power and money, to give it a common ideal that it is not a subjective whim. Nor are its ideals overly mystical, as can be seen in the great rational-idealist philosophical systems of Plato, the Upanishads, Hinduism (at least in some phases), the Christian philosophy of Thomas Aquinus, Nicolas of Cusa, Solovyov and of the medieval Arab philosopher Ibn-Khaldun, to name just a few. Its main inspiration is from human reason, but it admits the reality of matter and the senses also, and can balance within one consistent whole the evidence of the senses, of reason and the institutions of humankind in determining truth. In such a culture science, religion and philosophy are at peace with one another.

What can we do to encourage the emergence of such a culture? We should look for, and reinforce, the common idealistic elements already existing in Soviet and American (and other) societies and cultures. We should also look for and support the *idealists* already existing in Russian and American (and other) societies. The only open, public social group in the Soviet Union today truly independent of *nomenklatura* domination is the "Group for Trust," which was founded in June 1982 by a small group of idealistic artists and scientists (some of whom had formerly been refuseniks). It was for distributing their original "Appeal to the Governments and Publics of the USSR and USA" that Shatravka and Mishchenko were tried and sentenced (see above). Despite this, new people have joined the "peace group" faster than the authorities have arrested or deported them. Moreover, the arrests have made such an unfavorable impression on the Western peace movement that the "authorities" are apparently puzzled about just how best to deal with these "troublemakers."

The following excerpt from the *New York Times'* report on a large East-West peace conference held in Perugia, Italy, in July 1984 is illustrative:

> Mr. Lokshin (secretary of the Soviet Peace Committee) aroused anger with statements that there were no disarmament activists in the Soviet Union outside the official organization. He said that activists who have been imprisoned had been punished for "hooliganism" rather than their advocacy of disarmament. He was booed and heckled when he said that the "Trust Group," an unofficial disarmament body, was "supported by President Reason. . . . Public opinion and official opinion are the same in our society," he said to laughter. "They are always the same. We have ways of establishing this link.[21]

Many Western peace activists see the members of the "Trust Group" primarily as close personal friends. I will not try to speculate on their ultimate historical role (although the potential of it being significant is without doubt) except to point out that friendship (which does tend to thrive in an atmosphere of spiritual freedom, especially in the R.S.F.S.R.) plays a not at all insignificant role in the prevention of war, as does love in general.

The hoped-for new national/international society should start with small groups (cells, if you like) realizing these values at first in their social life, then in art and philosophy and then, as the cells coalesce into organs and the organs into a new (ideal-real) body, in legal, economic and productive life. Since an idealistic culture will have to contend with complex forces—including the "elemental," irrational and biological forces in any real society—specialized research in law, economics, political philosophy and other related fields must be given special attention from the very beginning.[22]

In economics I am convinced that first place must be given to the problem of developing social forms of production that allow the individual man or woman in society to produce not primarily for sale on the market, but for use by a meaningful social "familistic" (to use Sorokin's terminology) group. A "meaningful" group does not need to be identical with the family. One of the educational benefits of ethical positive law—as was pointed out by first Solovyov and then Petrazycki (who was much influenced by the great Russian philosopher)—is its tendency to expand our concept of meaningful and even "familistic" groups. For example, since slavery was outlawed the very idea of holding slaves has become repugnant to almost everyone, whereas in the past people in no sense our moral inferiors accepted it as "normal."[23]

Production "for sale" or "not for sale" is not a merely quantitative distinction, but refers primarily to the *intent* of production. It is particularly urgent to develop such forms of production in agriculture. Jane Jacobs' important work on the relation of the production of wealth to the creative diversity of the city suggests that agriculture of this type can only succeed in the urban or semi-urban environment, most likely the fringe of a medium or large city.[24] The importance of this idea is manifold, but perhaps the most obvious importance is that it could help defuse the explosive problem (and not only in Latin America and the Third World) of rural poverty, unemployment and the crisis of overproduction. Whereas socialism and, in the final analysis SuperStock, are mainly concerned with the redistribution of wealth, this approach focuses on its creation—but subject to idealistic requirements, such as Schumacher's "Beauty, Health and Permanence."

Steps taken toward the establishment of such an idealistic culture would improve the chances of American society implementing Super-Stock, but within the framework of an idealistic culture. As with much idealistic thought, the reasoning is dialectic. If we maintain our links with kindred spirits in the Soviet Union, the generation of peace may develop its own mutually reinforcing dialectic.

Editor's Comments

The paradox which Grenier points out is that despite all ideological appearances, the power elites in both America and Russia share the same basic value systems. Claiming that both elites have value systems geared to protect and extend their respective power bases implies that ideological convergence cannot bring disarmament in itself. So, Grenier, like Wisman, asserts that ideology validates existing institutions and disciplines a nation's citizens into accepting the power elite's claim to the privileges it enjoys.

Progress toward nuclear disarmament will naturally occur only if ideological convergence arises from the emergence of a dominant value system compatible with the tenets of peace. Krough's "interdependent" society and Grenier's "idealistic culture" embody this value system. Both Krough and Grenier claim that the needed value system already exists, but is subservient to that held by the dominant culture. To effect a transformation of societal values requires a transformation of individual values first, so both argue that change will flow from the bottom to the top. Emergence of a value system supportive of economic as well as political justice would eventually be articulated as a new ideology. Both essayists suggest that this new ideology would be compatible with theoretical Marxism.

If a Universal Share Ownership Plan is adopted early in the transformation process, would it enhance the emergence of the new culture? If Krough is correct in asserting the circular nature of the maturation process, then a USOP would enhance formation of the necessary values. Just as the institution of the family reinforces the emergence of interdependent human beings, the existence of the institution of a USOP would reinforce the emergence of interdependent human beings valuing economic democracy. This is consistent with either the Marxist position that institutions mold human consciousness or the alternative notion that institutions and individuals interact to shape one another.

Besides nurturing new values, Robert Whealey suggests that a USOP may ease tensions between the superpowers. In his essay he argues that the rhetoric of ideology clouds perceptions, leading to a breakdown in communication. Any type of national program that can be demonstrated to be compatible with Marxism would begin to undercut the rhetoric, to clear misperceptions and to build mutual trust. Grenier, on the other hand, suggests that without embrace of the values of an "idealistic culture," the impact of SuperStock would be similar to the central economic tenets of Marxism.

The Soviets may nonetheless have a positive reaction to America instituting a USOP. Mikhail Gorbachev has recently astonished Western observers with his appeals for "openness," "democracy," multi-candidate elections and economic reform. Whether he can succeed or not is secondary to the fact that the Politburo is experimenting with historically radical reform. The phenomenon of Gorbachev's appeals for reform reflects the long-realized need in Communist nations for ideological modernization. Instituting a USOP in the United States would suggest to the pragmatic Soviets that the US also recognizes the need for return on its economic and social system and might make it easier for them to accept Gorbachev's reforms. These reforms are all more democratic in nature and their existence is a necessary prerequisite for the emergence of a value system in the USSR compatible with lasting peace and political-economic democracy. In all this it is important to remember that what is necessary for permanently resolving the nuclear nightmare is that *both* nations evolve new value systems.

We can now ask whether or not the idea of equity-enhancing American economic reform is helped or hindered by linking it, as Speiser has done in his *Nuclear Nightmare* book, to nuclear disarmament and the achievement of greater ideological compatibility with the Soviet Union. Many essayists have argued that linking the USOP concept to nuclear disarmaments complicated the economic reform issue. They suggest that the USOP idea be decoupled from the peace issue and considered purely on its economic merits. Reflecting this view are the words of Jane Dillion from her essay "Selling SuperStock."

> Speiser must make a choice if he wants to do justice to his unusually promising economic plan. It may be true that using the nuclear nightmare in his title and presenting it as a central concern in his book are effective techniques in catching people's attention. It is likely that more people will respond to the question of how to end the nuclear nightmare than to the question of how to end the injustices of capitalism.

> By linking the issue of nuclear warfare with his attempt to find a solution to the inequities of US capitalism, however, Speiser is in fact doing a disservice to both issues. He is complicating the presentation of his economic plan and he is introducing emotionalism. The emotional "crusade" element can only confuse a rational analysis of that plan, thereby hindering a realistic commitment. People qualified to take a serious look at SuperStock are likely to be reluctant to believe claims that an adjustment to our economic system will end the nuclear arms race. Many think the nuclear war issue is more complicated than this. A tendency to dismiss both issues could result. On the other hand, people who become involved with Speiser's book because of an interest in the prevention of nuclear war could easily feel tricked by his attempt to attract their attention with the hopes of selling a new economic idea. Speiser would do better to disassociate these two issues and present his economic ideas as simply and clearly as possible.[25]

V.

LAND, RENT AND CAPITAL

Editor's Introduction

Ideological compatibility between Marxism and capitalism and coupling nuclear with disarmament with American economic reform are only two of several issues on which a number of essayists differed with Speiser or which they felt he overlooked. Another critical issue is reflected in this passage from the third volume of Marx's *Capital:*

> The fact that capitalized ground rent represents itself as the price value of land, so that the earth is bought or sold like any other commodity, serves to some apologists as a justification of private property in land, seeing that the buyer pays an equivalent for it, as he does for other commodities, and that the major portion of property in land has changed hands in this way. The same reason would, in that case, serve to justify slavery, since the returns from the labor of the slave, whom the slave-holder has bought, represent merely the interest on the capital invested in this purchase.[1]

Several essayists saw the lack of treatment of the land question as a serious omission by Speiser.

Fred Foldvary focused his essay contest paper, "Peace with Economic Justice," on the role land plays in our modern economy. He develops an alternative centered on the socialization of ground rent that he would introduce in addition to a USOP.

Contribution by Fred Foldvary

It is a great error to think that land was only important in earlier agricultural times, or in less developed countries. Even today, all wealth ultimately depends on land. Crops grow on land and all manufactures use raw materials from the land. All production takes place on land. People live on land. Even when people live and work in skyscrapers, they are not up in the clouds but on very expensive real estate—land. As long as our houses are not located in outer space, they sit on land which is ever more costly to obtain as the population keeps growing.

Land has become more, not less, important. Has the price of land generally gone up, or down? If land became less important, its relative price should have gone down. But everyone knows that real estate, or land, has for the most part gone ever upward in value.

Still, one could argue that although land is important, why not treat it as a different type of capital? The reason is that capital, as a product of human effort, derives its value mainly from the labor needed to produce it. But where does the land get its value, since nature produced it for free? Its value comes from its pure scarcity, from the fact that desirable land is a scarce resource in fixed supply. The owner of land did *nothing* to create its value! He obtains its value—the rent or the use of land—simply by being in *control* of that space, a control necessarily backed by the government.

Therefore, a key difference between capital and land is that the ownership of capital is earned by creating it, whereas the ownership of land is claimed only by government's recognition and enforcement of a land title giving the owner the legal right—actually a privilege—to control that space. . . .

Karl Marx wrote in *Capital* (Vol. 3): "In the absence of land monopoly, capital cannot exploit labor,"[2] since enough workers will go to free land to eliminate any labor surplus.

Once the good land is all claimed, the owners as a whole then have a de facto monopoly on the land. As the population grows, an ever greater share of the wealth goes as rent to the owners of land. We have seen this happening dramatically in recent years, as the proportion of the average family's income devoted to housing has been increasing and is now often one-third or more of family spending. Much of the gross earnings of business also goes to pay rent or mortgage payments.

The ultimate stopping point is the subsistence level, since if workers starve, the landlords cannot get any more rent. In fact, we see this very phenomenon operating in much of the Third World, where land ownership is highly concentrated and a privileged class of landowners lives from the rent paid by the masses of landless farmers and urban laborers.

Why has not rent absorbed the wealth of North American workers as it has in much of the rest of the world? Because the productive power of capital can offset this effect, at least for awhile. Technological progress has made capital so productive that labor's net earnings has increased and created a sizable middle class, despite the ever-increasing claim on wealth by rent. . . .

Why not apply Speiser's remedy—universal capitalism—to land? Create "universal landlordism" by making everyone an equal landowner!

How could we achieve this? The key is to realize that the benefit of land ownership is its rent. We do not need to physically redistribute land, as is badly done by most land reform programs. We need only divide up the rent of land. This can be accomplished by having all landowners pay rent, equal to the annual rental value of their land, to a common fund. This fund could then replace all taxes as the source of public revenues.

Would the land rent be enough to pay for the expense of all government levels? Steven Cord, an economist, has recently estimated that all land rent in the US came to $658 billion. In 1981, that amounted to 28 per cent of the national income and two-thirds of total government taxes.[3] Supplemented by user fees that could pay for many services, land rent would be enough to pay for all government programs. . . . Excess funds could be divided equally among the people. Universal landlordism would give everyone an equal share of the nation's natural resources and at the same time provide all the public revenues we need.

Without the public collection of land rent, a SuperStock plan would eventually be subject to the fatal flaw in primitive capitalism: land monopoly. If the poor suddenly had $10,000 per year in stock dividends, rents and land costs would rise until marginal workers were once again reduced to the subsistence level. The main benefit would be captured by the owners of land. But with universal landlordism, increased rents would flow back to the public, and the elimination of taxes on dividends would boost the benefits of Super-Stock even further. A plan for universal capitalism can only succeed on a foundation of the common ownership of land.

The public collection of land rent would lift the weight of disincentives we now place on enterprise and labor. Freed from income and sales taxes, enterprises would grow, providing jobs and lifting wages, with no need for artificial government stimulus, subsidies or "protection" from competition. Real wages would go up not just by eliminating taxes, but by the increasing demand for labor. There would be a further stimulus from driving underused or idle land into productive use and making more land available. Land would also be put to more efficient use, since land hogging, as is done in urban sprawl, would become more expensive. Finally, land speculation would be eliminated since the profit would be taken out of owning land, eliminating the business cycle and depressions. Universal landlordism plus universal capitalism would, as Speiser put it, combine "the emotional appeal of Marxism with the self-betterment drive and productive power of Adam Smith's laissez-faire,"[4] while preserving our liberties.

Would universal landlordism be fair to current landowners? First of all, just as it was recommended that SuperStock be implemented gradually, universal landlordism would best be implemented over a period of 15 years or so to minimize disruptions.

Owners of land would retain the rights of possession and would be able to buy and sell and use the land as they wished. Only the rental income from the land itself would be community property, not the use of the land or any improvements on it, such as buildings, fences, pools and crops.[5]

Thus, Foldvary argues that a USOP would be undermined by the inflationary impact it would have on land rents. His proposal would temper any induced inflation in real estate values and create a pool of funds for government financing with excess money being equitably disbursed to all Americans. Reading Foldvary's paper left the editor with many questions about his analysis, the details of his proposal, its relation to a USOP and its impact on different groups of economic actors.

A 100 per cent land rent tax may be compatible with the Constitution, yet even with a 15-year phase-in, the mere passage of required legislation would cause a collapse of certain land values and de facto confiscation of wealth from its owners.

Since ownership does not change, his proposal does not, as he claims, make "everyone an equal landowner." Like Speiser's USOP plan, Foldvary's 100 per cent land rent tax proposal redistributes income without effectively redistributing ownership, let alone control of productive assets which Wisman argues is crucial to building a more equitable economic order. Redistribution of ownership, which would violate the Constitution, was avoided by Speiser by targeting the distribution of capital formed in the future. Tomorrow may bring more capital, but it will not bring more land. No means exist to create a more equitable distribution of land ownership without violating the Constitution. Consequently, there is no way that American capitalism can be modified, within existing constraints, to remedy completely this Marxist objection. While Foldvary's analysis indicates that we can make some institutional modification which will treat the major abuses of concentrated land ownership, his proposal would not by itself bring about more widespread ownership.

Jeffrey Smith's essay contest paper, "Beyond Ideology and the Threat of Nuclear War—Geonomics," reflects the same spirit as Foldvary, but some of his comments clarify and strengthen the land rent issue. (Terms capitalized in the second and subsequent paragraphs signify their classical meanings.)

Contribution by Jeffrey Smith

Most people's income is diminished by four main drains: (1) Taxation—most people have to work from January until May in any given year to pay all their taxes. (2) Inflation—rising prices shrink the purchasing power of the dollar. (3) Unemployment—when people chase jobs, wages are low; when jobs chase people, wages are high. (4) Retention of rent from land.

This last drain, Rent retention, needs some explanation. Assume a mining operation, for example, that improves productivity by either discovering a richer deposit, or acquiring equipment that is faster and more automated, or boosting morale of employees with stock bonuses. Under any scenario, the Landholder can charge more Rent (if smart, the mining operator will be his own Landlord), but the Capital owner cannot charge more Interest (his price) and the

Laborers cannot charge more Wages. No matter what the business—shining shoes or making computers—any increase in productivity will benefit the Landholder, although he does nothing to create the increase. . . .

The Landholder's leverage is not obvious to most of us in the modern West where people have grown blind to the importance of Land. We are people who know food only as products on shelves in stores; we have lost touch with Land as the source of all Wealth. This was not always the case and still is not in the Third World, where Marxist promises of Land reform win large followings. Although little understood and largely ignored in Capitalist economies, Land Rent is the key to plugging all four drains. . . .

David Ricardo noted that a site's minimal value is fixed by its natural potential, but its maximal value is determined by its advantage over other sites that allow people, using the same Labor and Capital, to produce more and more quickly on one site versus another. That is, a site's worth is equal to the difference between its output (potential or actual) and that of the least productive sites in use, called the margin.

This difference in output is the Rent from that site; the Landlord can charge up to the amount that leaves the tenant as much as the Landless could produce on the worst usable Land available. The Landlord cannot charge more or the Landless would go to the margin; the Landlord would not charge less because that would not be acting in his self- interest.

Thus, Wages and Interest from any site are limited by what they would be on the margin. Therefore, the worse the worst site, the higher the Rent everywhere else, leaving less for Wages and Interest; and the better the worst site in use, the lower the Rent elsewhere, leaving more for Wages and Interest. So how the economic pie is divvied up is determined by first subtracting Rent, the value of Land, from the total output, then letting Capital and Labor haggle over the remainder.

The problem with Rent is not that it is so high or that it exists, but that it is retained by private claimants instead of collected by public agencies and used for public purposes. Were governments to collect Rent, they could afford not to tax. Doing so would be both fair and efficient; it would . . . (bring) capitalist distribution closer to justice. . . .

Besides upping distributive efficiency, abolishing taxes and collecting Rent also brings some sanity to tax policy. Adam Smith (who suggested collecting ground rent in his *Wealth of Nations*)[6] noted people bricking in windows or fireplaces, as Law taxed these items of Wealth. In general, taxes on Wealth make people save less; taxes on Labor make people work less; taxes on Capital make people invest less. Many people prefer continuing to use old, inefficient equipment rather than pay taxes on buying and owning new, more valuable technology. On the other hand, taxing Land (or "collecting ground Rent," or simply "Renting Land") impels people to use it to pay this fee.

Smith also suggested judging taxes for fairness (and effectiveness) by the following four standards. Ideally, a tax should: (1) include everyone without exemption or loophole; no one would feel safe in cheating nor be able to pass on their duty to another; (2) be proportional to benefit received; those who claim the most from society would pay back the most; (3) bear lightly on the production and distribution; business would go on at least as well as before; and (4) cost government little in being collected; mountains of paper work and armies of collectors would not be needed.

Ironically, tax has defects that Rent corrects; no tax meets all four standards: (1) an income tax encourages cheating; (2) a sales tax impedes trade and falls disproportionally on the poor; (3) a building tax is a discentive for improvement as it breeds sprawl and slums; (4) an inventory tax is hard to collect; etc.

On the other hand, charging Rent easily meets all four canons: (1) sites cannot be hidden nor their value disguised; (2) those enjoying the best locations can afford to pay the most; (3) the most valuable plots are put to highest and best use; and (4) government need not assess—a free market is constantly doing that—and can collect the Rent using only a portion of existing machinery while jettisoning the rest of bureaucracy. . . .

The idea of letting individuals keep earned income (Wages and Interest) and the community collect unearned income (Rent) was popularized over 100 years ago by Henry George in his seminal work, *Progress and Poverty*.[7] George reasoned this scheme is fair because Rent is from Land, which was made neither by nor for any one of us, yet is needed by all of us. Since we have a right to life, we have a right to live somewhere; we have a right to Land. Each of us has an equal right to this unequal resource.

Since Land varies in quality and is fixed in quantity, each site user should compensate everyone else excluded from his claim. Paying over Rent would either discourage hoarding and make more Land available, or compensate users of lesser sites. Collecting Rent would uphold our right to "trusterty," as ending taxes would uphold our right to property.

George's mechanism for accomplishing this compensation was a single tax on Land. This levy would be unique from all other taxes in that while taxes appear whenever rulers need money, Rent arises automatically whenever people produce Wealth on more than one grade of Land. A Rent levy does not fall on property—Wealth made or bought from its maker—but on trusterty—Land borrowed from its Maker. Its amount is not set arbitrarily by the State but fluctuates naturally with the value on Land. So the most occupants pay is not determined by governmental appetite but is limited by natural Law operating in a free market. Based on these differences, it is more accurate to say *not* "untax Labor and Capital and tax only Land," but "abolish all taxes and collect only Rent (at its full market value)," or more precisely, "let the community fund itself only by Renting all Land to its members."

The issue of Land ownership need not arise, since no title would be touched. Who owns a site is not important; who gets the Rent is. One person could own all Earth, or one Duke most of England, but if he paid all the ground rent to everyone else, he would have no advantage, and no non-owner would suffer. So claims to sites would stand as they are now. . . .

Paying social dividends from pooled ground Rent is both feasible and justifiable. Already, the nations of Saudi Arabia and Kuwait have no taxes; the State of Alaska returns dividends to its citizens from its oil revenue; and the Province of British Columbia pays out timber dividends. And these governments tap only one variety of Land value, resource Rent. . . .

To the extent we could export Rent reform to agrarian societies in the Third World (note that four-fifths of the world's two billion hungry are farmworkers), we could stave off bloody revolutions. Communism first took root in agrarian societies, instead of industrial ones as Marx predicted. Lenin's slogan was not "workers of the world unite" but "bread, peace and land." In China, Mao based his appeal on land to the peasants. In Vietnam, Ho and the Cong followed suit. Nicaraguan Sandinistans are the latest. Any nation succeeding in avoiding civil war and in attaining development for all classes via Rent reform would become an eternally grateful ally. . . . [8]

There were a number of essays that argued for some type of tax on land rent. The two just cited differ primarily in their views on how peace follows from their proposals. Foldvary argues that a USOP along with a 100 per cent land rent tax would create greater ideological compatibility and mutual trust for arms reduction negotiations between the superpowers. Smith's argument places exclusive emphasis on the land rent tax proposal and the exportation of "rent reform" to the Third World as the principal means for achieving global peace. He also believes that a 100 per cent land rent tax would be sufficient to create the climate between the US and USSR for dismantling the nuclear arsenals.

The relationship of land to capital is only one critical issue in American economic reform to promote a more just and democratic social order. We now turn our attention to plans for achieving these goals through greatly expanded, if not universal, ownership of capital.

VI.

FINE-TUNING THE CONCEPT OF UNIVERSAL CAPITALISM

Editor's Introduction

The idea of state intervention in modern economic life goes back at least a century to Gladstone and Disraeli in England and Bismarck in Germany. The welfare state, in which governments use taxes, transfers and other programs to raise the living standards of the poor, was introduced to the United States during the Franklin D. Roosevelt administration in the 1930s and accelerated three decades later during Lyndon Johnson's presidency. For a host of reasons, by the end of the 1970s the welfare state began to be seen by many as inherently dysfunctional and came under attack during the conservative presidency of Ronald Reagan. He mounted in the 1980s a systematic attack on the social welfare programs built up over one-half of a century. Yet the question the welfare state sought to answer remains: how can we deal with the inherent lack of economic equality which capitalism naturally creates?

When one scans the options available to potentially answer this essential question, the concept of a USOP stands out. Arthur Okun once stated: "[The conflict] between equality and efficiency [is] our biggest socioeconomic tradeoff, and it plagues us in dozens of dimensions of social policy. We can't have our cake of market efficiency and share it equally."[1]

The belief imbedded in this quotation is in large part a result of the failed social policies of the past. The beauty of the concept of greatly expanded and more equitable ownership of productive assets is that it seems to refute this notion that equality and efficiency are basically contradictory. Designed properly, a Universal Share Ownership Plan may promote both efficiency and equity in the American economy. Once the American public again becomes aware of the dangers associated with growing economic inequality, the compelling logic of a correctly constructed USOP will draw a forceful constituency.

The current approach to the social problems which arise from poverty is a second-best solution. What we need is a first-best solution which will provide more jobs, enhance incentives to work and create a more egalitarian distribution of earnings. As long as an economy experiences rapidly growing productivity, the search for a first-best solution, which may involve some difficult choices, can be avoided. Once a nation begins having low productivity growth, it becomes impossible to avoid equity questions.

In seeking a first-best solution one must realize that equity is not synonymous with equality. Equity exists when everyone is treated fairly. What constitutes fair treatment is not constant but rather changes over time. In American society today an increase in fair treatment would include, among other features, a more equal distribution of economic opportunity. Widespread access to the opportunities enjoyed by a small handful today would unleash incentives across a broad spectrum of Americans to strive to become "elites of merit." Productivity would rise and economic growth would follow. Thus, to use Lester Thurow's words, "equity is the essence of efficiency."[2]

The editor's own submission in the essay contest seeks to address the equity/efficiency dilemma within a broader examination of social problems than undertaken by Speiser. It also explores modifications in the American economic system toward attainment of ideological compatibility as well as proposes changes in Speiser's Universal Share Ownership Plan to make it more efficient and effective.

The Alpha Proposal

by Kenneth B. Taylor[3]

... I see the same blackness, hear the same thunder, see the same lightning everyone else does. But I ascribe this not to the end, but to the beginning. I see the dangers we face now as part of the process of evolution, which I see as a survival mechanism. I see the possibility for human beings to evolve to a new stage; to respond consciously to the threats to our survival, to do something about our survival and not leave it entirely to chance.

—Jonas Salk

The American Dilemma

Historically, America's problems were primarily external and easy to identify. Most came in the form of disease, natural disasters and the aggressive actions of ambitious rulers and their armies. Today the most persistent and dangerous crises we face on the whole stem from within. More important, our current problems have largely positive rather than negative origins. In other words, the crises which we now face were created by people acting with the best of intentions.[4]

So that an increasing number of people could enjoy a rising standard of living, our ancestors turned the machinery of the Industrial Revolution loose in the land. In the process of generating more wealth we despoiled the land, polluted our environment and inequitably distributed the rising standard of living among the people.

To eliminate dangerous or undesirable jobs and to enhance the profits of industry, we introduced machines at all levels of employment and have done so at an increasing rate over time. Two negative results have been a rising average level of absolute unemployment, as well as unemployment as a percentage of the total labor force. As we have substituted mechanical for metabolic energy, this process has also contributed to pollution and the rapid depletion of natural resources.

In order to prolong life and reduce human suffering we have poured billions of dollars into medical research and facilities. Conquering disease is universally supported and much progress has been made toward attainment of this goal. Unfortunately, there is even a dark side to this noble endeavor. In reducing the incidence of disease and prolonging life we have unleased a population explosion in the world. Modern science, conquering disease faster than increasing the food supply, has kept people from dying from germs only to confront them with death from famine as insufficient supplies of food develop. Here in America demographers assure us that this is one problem which will bypass us. Yet we should not deceive ourselves; for even if this problem does not directly concern us, there will be no escaping the indirect impact of overpopulation in our increasingly interwoven world (e.g. revolutions, terrorism, famine, international debt and so forth.)

With the objective of ending the Second World War and in many hopeful minds war for all time, we invented the supreme deadly weapon: the nuclear bomb. It may be said that nuclear weapons have played a major role in preventing the Third World War during the past four decades. Yet the price we have paid has been, and will continue to be, high. Every time we build a weapon we create a product which will never contribute to economic growth. A weapon is not like an industrial machine which will go on producing goods and thus generating income once it has been created. The billions spent on the nuclear arms race have dampened the growth rate of our Gross National Product (GNP) as well as the rate at which we create more jobs for our citizens. One study of major industrial countries showed that the two nations, which over the course of the past 20 years spent the greatest percentage of their GNP on military expenses—the United States and Great Britain—also had the slowest rates of productivity growth. On the other hand, the two nations that had the highest rates of growth—Japan and Denmark— spent the lowest percentage of their GNPs on the military.[5]

Nuclear weapons have changed the landscape of international politics to a degree unparalleled by any other peacetime factor in history. The nuclear confrontation has made us all prisoners of a worldwide existential hell. Fear and alienation undermine the collective psyche of society, injecting paranoia into the way we view many foreigners as well as some of our fellow citizens.

The existence of nuclear weapons has seemed to create the preconditions for their use. All this forms a closed circle of fear and hostility.

Crises of these magnitudes are always rooted in history. Yet who do we justly blame? Many argue that today's crises were created by beliefs. As Mesarovic and Pestel pointed out in *Mankind at the Turning Point:* "Today it seems that the basic values, which are ingrained in human societies of all ideologies and religious persuasions, are ultimately responsible for many of our troubles."[6] The crises confronting America are logical consequences of the prevailing culture and traditional concept of progress. To deal with our collective predicament we need to change our way of thinking. The institutional modifications which will result, rather than serving individuals at the expense of the common goal, must put bread on our unemployed neighbor's table and leave a clean, prosperous and peaceful world for our children to inherit.

The Forces of Change

The Limits to Growth, written by Meadows, Meadows, Randers and Behrens and published in 1972, purported to weave together the forces behind the trends described earlier and herald imminent global disaster in comprehensive analytical detail.[7] Critics of this treatise were abundant and quick to react. In retrospect these critics served an important role in defining what the founder of the Club of Rome, Aurelio Peccei, called the "world problematique." After over a decade of careful scientific scrutiny certain trends outlined in *The Limits to Growth* are still supported. In regard to pollution Thomas Jones concludes that the authors had an unchallengeable point: "They perceive that natural delays in ecological processes (the extended time required for some pollutants to exert their full environmental impact) increase the likelihood that necessary control measures will be underestimated."[8] A pollution-precipitated disaster could limit industrial growth by diverting an exorbitant share of national income to pay for environmental, social and personal costs. After reviewing the literature engendered by *The Limits to Growth* on the issues of potential food production and population growth projections, Jones is also compelled to agree with the book's advocacy of global population stabilization: "To facilitate efforts to provide nourishing food for everyone, tandem efforts must be made to stabilize the world's population at as low a level as is compatible with acceptable means."[9]

The growth processes studied in *The Limits to Growth* assumed an exponential growth pattern. One of the most topical examples of a process exhibiting this type of growth is cancer. Once a cancerous cell establishes itself, it will continue to reproduce itself without limit. Once metastasized, it will eventually develop to the point where it inhibits the functioning of vital organs, often killing its host. The parallel between this example and conclusion of *The Limits of Growth* that population and industrial output growth will eventually kill modern industrial civilization is not coincidental. Any process exhibiting exponential growth within a closed system, the human body or the earth, must eventually reach a limit and extinguish itself. In the second report to the Club of Rome, Mihajlo Mesarovic and Edward Pestel asserted that it is an irrefutable diagnosis that we are coming to an end of a period of exponential growth.[10] Assuming an economic growth rate of 5 per cent per year, at the end of the next century America's GNP would be 500 times greater than it is today. The issue of depletion of scarce resources notwithstanding, the problems of acquiring, processing and disposing of materials would be impossible to solve.

The Mesarovic-Pestel analysis argues that the growth process reflected by organic life is the only realistic one for the world processes to be following. This differentiated or organic growth process can be represented graphically as a logistic growth curve (Figure 5). There are two specific phases of growth in this type of process. The first is from "t" to α (alpha) and is locally characterized by exponential growth. The second phase, from α to β (beta), can be said to display a gradual slowing down of growth with the rate of growth becoming zero at beta. This illustration is a mathematically pure statement, whereas the real world will display many discontinuities and aberrations depending on the process in question and the state of all related variables. This point will be important in a later discussion and means that in the real world the inflection point alpha and maximum point beta are not specific points but rather fuzzy intervals along the time axis. Some students of the subject support the point of view which contends that the United States entered the transition interval, represented by alpha, during the decade of the 1970s. During the decade of the 1950s economic growth in this country averaged 3.8 percent, during the 1960s the average increased to 4.0 per cent and finally for the decade of the 1970s growth fell to an average of 3.6 percent. This slowing down of economic growth could very well indicate that the transition has begun.

Figure 5

LOGISTIC GROWTH

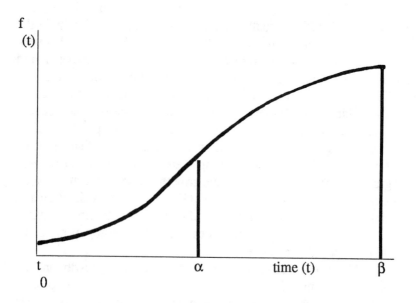

Reinforcement of this notion that economic growth must slow down is found in the study of Entropy Economics. Many social scientists have claimed that the laws of economics must respect those of nature and physics. Paul Samuelson has said: "You can't make a perpetual motion machine that will run by a dropped ball's bouncing back to higher than its point of release. That's a consequence of the first law of thermodynamics—which guarantees conservation (or constancy) of the total energy."[11] More important here is the implication of the second law of thermodynamics which states that the total entropy (disorder) of a system irreversibly increases when the total energy remains constant. Using Samuelson's analogy of a bouncing ball, this means that the height of the ball on each subsequent bounce will be less and less. Considering the global economy as a closed energy system leads one to conclude that economic activity (growth) must slow down. One would expect the epitome of economic growth, the American economy, to be among the first to reflect this fundamental law of nature.

If one accepts organic growth as the true growth pattern present in the industrial and population processes, then one begins to wonder about the implications. In other words, what is in store for America between alpha and beta? Lester Thurow has written on the implications of zero economic growth in his book, *The Zero-Sum Society*. Although he postulates a scenario where no economic growth is present, his insights are applicable to the time interval between alpha and beta, where the rate of growth begins to slow down, finally equaling zero. When an economy is growing rapidly there is no concerted cry for economic equality. As the pie (GNP) gets bigger, everyone's piece (disposable income) can conceivably grow. When the pie stops growing, people would begin to fight over their particular slice to keep the American dream of a rising standard of living alive. But, as Thurow points out, zero economic growth does not have the same impact on all people. Therefore, even without fighting over shares of the pie, subtle structural mechanisms are present which will alter the distribution of income. Unfortunately, the already existing inequalities in income distribution would be magnified. Thurow looks at the gap between families who are at the 25th percentile of the population and those who are at the 75th percentile. Given zero economic growth,

> . . . this interquartile range rises by about .2 per cent per year for whites and 2.3 per cent per year for blacks. Since unemployment and reduced employment opportunities strike blacks harder than whites, inequality in black income distribution increases at a faster rate than that for whites. Moreover, black family incomes fall relative to those

of whites by about 6.5 per cent per year.[12]

Not only would the distribution of income between whites and blacks worsen, it would worsen between men and women and between older and younger workers as well.[13] With labor force growth rates in excess of economic growth rates, an additional consequence would be an increasing overall unemployment rate. This scenario would necessarily mean a declining per capita GNP and, consequently, a falling standard of living. In the final analysis those hurt most by slower growth will be minorities, women and the young.

Reinforcing this increased economic inequality will be two more structural characteristics of the American economic system. Creel Froman points out that, "contrary to general myth, one does not become wealthy through saving."[14] One of the two ways to become wealthy, or more realistically to magnify existing wealth, is through capital investment. This basically means that by investing in, or arranging debt financing for, a new business which turns out to be successful, one can sell one's stake in this business at a later date at the present value of all future cash flows associated with that investment. For a truly successful business, this could leave the original investor many times wealthier. Although this wealth-creating avenue is open to anyone with the proper drive and ingenuity, the people who in fact have the money to finance such investments, or support themselves during the time it takes to make a business successful, are those already possessing considerable wealth. These people would be the 19 per cent of the population who currently own 76.2 per cent of all American wealth and their heirs. This wealth-generating vehicle is operative whether or not the economy as a whole is growing. It would further serve to accentuate the inequality in the distribution of wealth and income between the haves and have-nots during a time of slowing economic growth.

Inheriting wealth is the second major way to get wealthy. As Froman states in his book: "Most economists agree that inherited wealth serves no economic function. That is, inheritances are very good for those who inherit them, but they are neither necessary nor even good for the economy."[15] Within the context of a decelerating economy, the institution of inheritance would serve as a support structure for the processes outlined above.

None of the works mentioned thus far addresses the nuclear crisis as an integral part of our total predicament. This is unfortunate since the nuclear confrontation between the superpowers is as related to the Industrial Revolution as is the depletion of natural resources, pollution and overpopulation. It was the socioeconomic processes emerging in the context of the Industrial Revolution which led Karl Marx to conclude that the owners of the means of production, the capitalists, were exploiting the vast majority of the population comprising the working class. The Soviet regime was founded on Marxist ideology and maintains control to a large degree through this ideology. It has been said that ever since the Bolshevik Revolution of 1917, the course of history has been played out as a clash of "irreconcilable ideologies."[16] Nuclear weapons have become the fearful symbol of the conflict between capitalism and communism.

In sum, America is harnessed to a capitalist economic engine which common sense tells us must slow down; has a polluted environment which only seems to be getting worse; and has thousands of nuclear weapons in a military establishment that drains billions of dollars from productive investments every year and which keeps the global ideological conflict in an uneasy draw. America operates internationally in an environment where a population time bomb is ticking. At home America is experiencing soaring national debt. Add to this the observation that as our economy slows down, as economic inequality increases, as millions more Americans fall below the poverty level, the threat of socialist revolution or reactionary fascism from within increases.

All of this defines the broad contours of the future if we sit idly by and do nothing. These may seem to present intractable problems. Yet if we are willing to take the long view of things, bold enough to open our minds and brave enough to take action, solutions which will preserve democracy and our basic freedoms exist. As Lester Thurow pointed out: "Intractable problems are usually not intractable because there are no solutions, but because there are no solutions without severe side effects."[17] Herein lies our challenge: To create solutions which are consistent with democratic principles and which have a minimum of long-term side effects.

The Alpha Proposal

In his book, *How to End the Nuclear Nightmare,* Stuart Speiser presents a persuasive argument for why the Soviets cannot be expected to address the ideological conflict in a way that will ease tensions between the superpowers.[18] Furthermore, he states:

> Our economic system, in contrast, is much more flexible. Unlike Soviet communism, American capitalism is not defined or even mentioned in our Constitution or laws. We Americans, moreover, have greater power to influence our government. We are free to take a fresh

look at capitalism and determine whether it can be made more compatible with communism. It is, therefore, up to us to take that first step toward ideological accord.[19]

Speiser further contends that we have been trying desperately to save capitalism since the great depression through the concept of "welfare capitalism":

> ... our Band-Aid remedies are no longer working, precisely because they are not sweeping enough; they provide only temporary relief from symptoms while ignoring the disease itself—the widening gap between capitalists and non-capitalists.[20]

He believes, therefore, that the principal flaw in the long-term survivability of American capitalism is the increasingly unequal distribution of income and wealth.

The inflation and economic stagnation of the 1970s created the perception of, and in many instances the reality of, declining standards of living. Under these widespread circumstances, those employed took a hard look at their paychecks and began to get angry at the share going to government. As was mentioned earlier, in a time of prosperity welfare capitalism can work since the general standard of living improves, despite rising taxes. Few complain as long as after-tax income is growing. In a sense then the tax revolt movement of the early 1980s indicates that the fighting over the shares of the pie has begun, with Uncle Sam's piece the first to shrink.

The political events of the early 1980s in connection with the Federal Reserve's decisive move to reduce inflation created the false impression that what had gone wrong in the 1970s was made right in the 1980s. With this mentality, government, business and private consumers piled up historically high debt on a spending spree. By spending beyond our income we created an economic boom, but one with a hollow core. It was fueled with more borrowed money than any other expansion since the Second World War.

From all economic indicators it would seem that America has not yet entered the alpha interval, but this is true in appearances only. The day will come when we or our children will have to pay for our current illusions. If the public debt continues to accumulate at the current rate, it will reach $3 trillion by the early 1990s.[21] Disregarding for the present the long-term influence this may have on interest rates and consequently economic activity, the impact on the ability of government to purchase public goods out of current tax revenues will become significant. For every tax dollar received in 1984, 17 cents went to pay interest on the national debt. This is a rise from 7 cents per tax dollar in 1974. As the public debt increases, a shrinking portion of each current tax dollar is left over to purchase public goods and services. Richard Everett, domestic economist for Chase Manhattan Bank, has added that, "There is a disturbing prospect that the government's interest payments will soon be equal to the annual deficit. At that point, the debt will take on a life of its own. . . ."[22] The above were created as a consequence of the effort to keep capitalism going while denying the facts that our economy has matured and growth is slowing down. Not surprisingly, the economic remedies we have introduced have only made our socioeconomic system more diseased. The cure will be all the more painful once we face reality.

Tracing many of America's economic and ideological problems back to the inequitable distribution of income and wealth, Speiser advocates a new allocation mechanism for the means of production—SuperStock.[23] The essential features of this mechanism have been described in the first chapter. The end result would be to create ". . . a system of equitable income distribution based on the strength of capitalism—the ability of productive capital to pay for itself—rather than on the weaknesses inherent in government welfare handouts."[24]

We could dispute the details of this plan, but let us stand back and assess the merits of the SuperStock proposal in light of our earlier discussion. Speiser's explicit hope in seeing SuperStock introduced is to reduce the ideological hostilities between the superpowers. A reduction in tensions would be a direct result of the Kremlin's perception that SuperStock eliminates their primary ideological point of contention with capitalism: the ownership of the means of production by a minority of individuals. Speiser does point out that the Kremlin retains power in large part by the "external threat," so that making capitalism compatible with Marxist theory may not in itself reduce tensions. Still, eliminating the ideological basis for the superpowers' confrontation is unquestionably a step in the right direction. At least it addressed the underlying reason for the nuclear arms race—namely, the conflict between the US and USSR.

But does the SuperStock plan outlined by Speiser truly represent the dissemination of the means of production to all citizens? Economists have argued that ownership and property rights are not synonymous. In the long run control over property is more important than ownership. According to Speiser's plan, the symbol of ownership, shares of stock in corporations, will be widely held. Yet control of the property these shares represent will rest in the traditional hands of management and holders of existing common stock. On this basis alone, Marxist theorists would contend that SuperStock is no more than a ploy on the part of capitalists to fool the working class into thinking they have control over the means of production.

In the Speiser plan the recipient of SuperStock has neither voting power in corporate decisions nor power to sell shares of SuperStock. To distribute both ownership and control widely, SuperStock must be both votable and tradeable. Speiser worries that if SuperStock is made voting stock, there would be a change in the control of corporations and the possible destruction of the business skills which have developed over time.[25] Given how widely SuperStock would be distributed, the number of shares involved and the cost associated with garnering support, it seems reasonable to assume that the only time sufficient votes could be amassed to turn out the management of a corporation would be in the instance where there was good reason for change. There appears to be no basis to assume that SuperStockholders would behave less prudently than common shareholders. Also, as Speiser admits, "No doubt the SuperStockholders would have a stronger feeling of participation in capitalism if they could vote and sell their shares or borrow against them. . . ."[26]

Admittedly, if SuperStock could be exchanged publicly, it would have a devastating effect on the prices at which the stock of these 2,000 corporations were traded. Still, it is important that the SuperStockholder be able to trade in or borrow against the shares they own. The driving force behind entrepreneurship, and thus economic growth in America, is individual innovation and invention. Allowing a person to place his wealth, including SuperStock, behind his ideas is an important element in fostering future economic activity. Those people who are willing to take on risk should be encouraged in all ways possible. So that the stock markets are not depressed by an inundation of SuperStock, legislation setting up the program should specify that a holder of SuperStock may sell his shares back to the government at either the value of the shares at time of issuance or current market values, whichever is lower. This will allow a holder to liquidate his shares but not at the government's expense. Returned shares will be treated as new investment, being held in escrow until the stream of dividends pays for the transaction and then redistributed by a formula to be described shortly.

A SuperStock mutual fund will no longer work under this revised plan. The "bundle" of SuperStock shares issued to eligible recipients will now be in the form of a portfolio where risk has been diversified as much as possible. By making SuperStock voting stock and by giving the holder the right to borrow against or cash in shares, the plan goes a greater distance toward eliminating the Marxist ideological objection to capitalism. At the same time, once a holder can tap the purchasing power of his SuperStock shares, the entrepreneurial spirit, if it exists in the holder, will be kindled and at least partially financed.

Marxists may still find another objection to this revised plan due to the existing unequal distribution of wealth at the onset of the program. As was argued in the preceding section, mechanisms are structured into capitalism which give the already rich a much greater money earning capacity for their wealth. One must ask the question of whether or not Speiser's SuperStock plan will significantly narrow the gap in the distribution of income and wealth. Speiser states that:

> ... according to reliable projections, American business will create at least $5 trillion worth of new capital over the next 20 or so years. If that figure is divided among the 50 million households who presently own little or no capital, each household would receive $100,000 worth of SuperStock. ... And at the current pre-tax return rate of 20 per cent on invested capital, each household could expect to receive about $20,000 (a year) in dividends. ...[27]

Several qualifying comments are in order. First, this statement is based on the assumption of constant economic growth. But there is good reason to believe that economic growth will slow down in the future. If so, then the creation of $5 trillion of new capital over the next 20 years is unrealistically high. This would put less SuperStock, and consequently smaller dividends, into the hands of those who presently own little or no capital. Second, the current pre-tax return rate of 20 per cent on invested capital is based on the current financial leveraging practice employed by American business. Eliminating the use of debt and retained earnings by the participating corporations will eliminate leverage as a means for magnifying the return on equity. Therefore, the actual pre-tax return on capital may well be a fraction of the current rate. This means that SuperStockholders will likely receive considerably less dividend income than Speiser projects, regardless of the dollar value of the SuperStock shares they own. All this sets the stage for continued inequitable distribution of wealth and income in America.

Before suggesting a second structural change in American capitalism which can deal with this problem, we must first ask two more questions. How does SuperStock propose to deal with the problem of environmental pollution? Will SuperStock help our children deal with the enormous national debt we are going to pass on to them?

First, the SuperStock proposal outlined by Speiser in no way addresses the issue of pollution. Consequently, the possible scenario of having an exorbitant proportion of income and wealth diverted to deal with environmental decay in the future is ignored. If this contingency materializes, SuperStock would stall since new capital investments and dividends would decline and possibly approach zero.

Second, Speiser's SuperStock plan does not directly address the issue of the public debt. The presumption is either that the public debt will not affect future economic activity or that the economic growth of tomorrow will generate a surplus of government revenue which will make retirement of the public debt feasible. The economic theory which states that as the national debt grows the servicing of this debt will "crowd out" private borrowing in capital markets by boosting interest rates is well known. If this theory is correct, the long-term consequences of a titanic, perpetual public debt will be high real interest rates and depressed private capital investment and economic growth. It was mentioned earlier that as the interest rate payments on the public debt grow relative to tax revenue, each tax dollar will purchase less government goods and services. So we face the very real prospect of paying the same or greater taxes, yet receiving less and less current public goods and services. In effect, we will be paying for public goods and services which were bought and consumed yesterday.

Inheritance is wealth which was created from the flow of past income—that is, income which was earned when prices did not reflect the cost of the pollutants which were spilling into the environment and when tax revenues were too low to pay for the public goods and services being provided. For these reasons a 100 per cent inheritance tax needs to be introduced in tandem with SuperStock. One portion of inheritance tax revenues should go to cleaning up the pollution resulting from past production and consumption. This must be coupled with stringent legislation aimed at controlling ongoing pollution. It has been argued that if pollution controls are well thought out and implemented, they need not dampen economic growth.[28]

Another portion of inheritance tax revenues should go toward retirement of the public debt. Reducing the national debt should be done prudently so that its economic effects are neutral or counter-cyclical. All SuperStock shares which are acquired by the government through the inheritance tax should be transferred to the SuperStock fund for redistribution.

Finally, the 100 per cent inheritance tax will have the effect of eliminating most of the built-in structural inequality in the distribution of income and wealth. Since we will all start economically more or less equal, equality of opportunity will be more of a fact in American life. Any remaining economic inequality will be the direct result of varying individual effort, skill and luck. This should help considerably in reducing the tensions between groups and between individuals as economic growth continues to slow. To enhance individual motivation, it is important that people be able to keep as much as possible from the current income they earn. Toward this end, once the public debt is retired, and past pollution cleaned up, inheritance tax revenues should be transferred to the general revenue fund, allowing for all other taxes to be reduced. Eliminating the structural basis of economic inequality will also silence the remaining ideological point of contention with Marxists, thereby laying a more complete foundation for the reduction in tensions between the superpowers.

A 100 per cent inheritance tax will also affect the issue of eligibility for participation in SuperStock. It is proposed here that all American citizens be eligible and receive their portfolio of SuperStock upon attaining the age of 18. The dollar value of the portfolio received will be equal to the average annual value of new capital investment by the participating corporations over the past 18 years, divided by the average annual national birthrate for the same period. This formula will smooth out the effects of both economic and demographic fluctuations over a long period of time, permitting a more equitable intergenerational distribution of SuperStock shares.

Unlike the Speiser plan, which recommends at least a seven-year phase-in, this current proposal implicitly assumes an 18-year phase-in. Given that economic growth slows down and the dividend payout is not as high as Speiser predicts, it may very well take an average of 18 years for the debt incurred in initially creating SuperStock shares to be paid off. All the while, as Speiser says, "We would have to keep our Social Security and welfare programs alive, at least temporarily, to cover those who did not become eligible for SuperStock."[29] It will take, therefore, at least a generation to dismantle the colossal social welfare apparatus we have created.

One last factor could potentially reduce the viability of any Super-Stock plan and leads to a third structural change to be included to complete the Alpha Proposal. Given America's traditional open-door policy on immigration and the existence of theories stating that the decline in the US population growth rate may not be permanent, a disturbing possibility emerges.[30] If the US population growth rate exceeds the economic growth rate over the long term, the value of SuperStock portfolios (and consequently derived dividend income) will fall over time. One result could be that the dividend income yielded, and indeed the cash value of the portfolio itself, may not be sufficient to provide a subsistence existence for an unemployed owner. It may be argued that this is not a highly probable scenario for America. However, if our modification of capitalism is to be a model for other capitalist nations, of which many do have serious population problems, this issue must be addressed at the time the Alpha Proposal is implemented.

The basis for this last potential scenario can be understood through the discussion of two economic laws: The law of the increasing returns to scale and the law of diminishing returns. With a given amount of natural resources and capital, a growing population results in a faster growth in economic output. One important consequence is rising output per person or average standard of living. Beyond a certain point, the law of diminishing returns sets in: When there are too many hands relative to available physical capital and natural resource, output per person and the standard of living falls. This last possibility is what is envisioned happening in the scenario described above. These facts are shown graphically in Figure 6.

Figure 6

OPTIMUM POPULATION

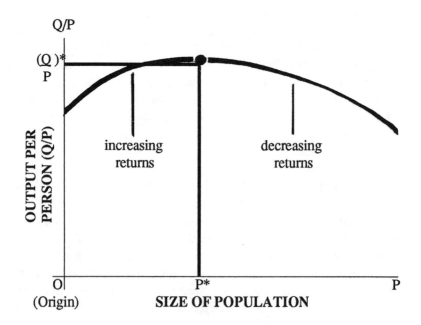

Up to point P*, increasing returns-to-scale dominate the economy and population growth results in an increasing standard of living. But beyond this point, decreasing returns dominate and living standards plummet. As the graph clearly shows, there exists an optimum population, P*, where output per person is maximized. So that American citizens receive the highest average standard of living our economy can provide, it is proposed that legislation be introduced with the aim of attaining the optimum national population. This goal need not be achieved coercively. Along with educational programs, we could build incentive schemes where, for instance, parents having only two children are given an additional allocation of SuperStock shares when their second child reaches 18 years of age. There exist many positive incentive plans which would be compatible with our laws and social mores.

It has been noted that economists would be unable to pinpoint exactly what the optimum population level would be.[31] Still, there is no doubt that researchers could designate a narrow range of population levels with a high probability of containing the optimum level. Since the type of population program suggested here would not result in an exact population level anyway, a targeted range would be adequate. Finally, as time progresses, the underlying factors affecting the optimal population will change so that continuous reassessment of this optimum will be required. As the optimum changes, the population stabilization programs can be stepped-up or eased accordingly.

Beta and Beyond

Where there is no vision the people perish.

—Proverbs 29:18

Increased depletion of scarce resources was not addressed in the Alpha Proposal. Despite warnings to the contrary, we will never run out of any natural resource. Most researchers of this genre have ignored the power of the price mechanism, if unimpeded, to regulate the relative and absolute scarcity of natural resources. As a resource becomes increasingly scarce, its relative price will rise. Differential price changes across all natural resources will reduce demand, encourage substitutions and thereby relieve shortages. This does not contradict the American experience with oil in the mid-1970s. OPEC's oil embargo represented an abrupt disruption of oil supplies within highly regulated markets. One lesson learned from this experience was that the workings of our economy could be seriously disrupted by external forces.

This brings us to the issue of the role of government during the transition from alpha to beta. Robert Heilbroner believes that all the tensions wrought by a declining growth economy will necessitate increased government intervention.[32] The Alpha Proposal is aimed at making a limited number of initial changes in our socioeconomic system, while preserving decentralized government and the potential for flexible response by government to specific short-term crises which may arise over time. After a period of intense intervention as the Alpha Proposal legislation is passed, government will return to its more traditional role.

Some students of capitalism rely on the introduction of new technologies to continue fueling economic growth and preserving the present American system.[33] New technologies, it is argued, will emerge allowing us to clean up the environment cheaply and to create substitute resources for those currently being depleted. What they say is conceivable yet by no means guaranteed. A principal flaw in the "Technofix" solution is that it fails to deal with critical social issues. Primarily, it fails to address the inequitable distribution of wealth and income both domestically and internationally.

The inequitable distribution of wealth and income between the have and have-not nations has a worrisome long-run potential. Observing the population growth rates in many less developed countries, Heilbroner envisions a scenario of population overload, poverty, famine and socioeconomic collapse.[34] Tyrannical dictators may emerge from this social disintegration, seeing the industrialized nations as having enriched themselves by using the labor power and resources of the less developed nations. We tend to worry about the nuclear confrontation between the US and the USSR when, in the long run, the nuclear confrontation may very well be broader. Nuclear weapons in the hands of such a dictator with such beliefs may precipitate the use of these weapons as an instrument to exact a massive transfer of wealth to a less developed nation. The point here is really three-fold: The "Technofix" solution ignores the underlying ideological conflict of the nuclear nightmare, the general conflict between the haves and have-nots of the world and the economic mechanisms which have created and sustain the gulf between the two.

The Alpha Proposal seeks to address the major socioeconomic conflicts of the times. By introducing SuperStock, wealth and income can become more evenly distributed across the population. At the same time, we will be introducing an antidote to our anemic social welfare system, building an institution which will help ease the inevitable conflicts which will arise between various social groups as economic growth slows down, and removing a principal ideological barrier between communism and capitalism (ownership of the means of production). The need to tap the nation's stock of wealth (accumulated past income) follows logically from the facts that the stock of pollution in our environment and America's immense national debt were created in the past. A 100 per cent inheritance tax will provide the funds to liquidate these debts as well as to remove the major structural basis for intergenerational economic inequality.

Given our deeply rooted desire to protect life while maintaining the quality of life, a population stabilization program—will preserve the intent of the first two parts of the Alpha Proposal by protecting them from being undermined by excessive population growth. By making these three systemic adjustments, America will set an example of how a capitalist democracy can attain greater socioeconomic equity, a high standard of living despite slow economic growth and a clean, healthy environment while maintaining basic liberties.

The Communist nations' responses to these changes, and the ideological conflicts they address, will strip them to the nakedness of their true political intent and lack of dedication to world peace. Blatant despotism will no longer hide behind the guise of "dictatorship of the proletariat" and the world's people will judge each nation by their efforts to reduce the nuclear confrontation and treat their citizens justly. The Alpha Proposal may not resolve the inequitable distribution of wealth or income among nations, but available evidence suggests that the Marxist and "Technofix" capitalist paths are even less likely to bridge the gap.

As a parting note, readers may have wondered what is in store for America beyond the beta point. Figure 1 is only a two- dimensional representation of an enormously complex phenomenon. It therefore does not imply socioeconomic stagnation or decline after beta. As Daniel Bell and a host of others have pointed out, the history of civilization shows a clear pattern of logistic growth cycles.[35] Each cycle tends to be dominated by a certain axial force born of specific innovations in societal technology during the previous cycle. Many feel that the current innovation in societal technology centers on information storage, manipulation and dissemination, and that it can be expected to cause fundamental changes resulting in a social paradigm shift. Thus, like the legendary Phoenix rising from the ashes, civilization can reemerge to grow again in some new form.

It is not for us to judge whether changes in information technology will provide the axial force of the next cycle, nor to hypothesize about the socioeconomic problems that will need to be addressed beyond beta. These are the questions for a future generation. Our obligation is to confront today's crises and societal inequities with all the wisdom and force we can gather. Toward fulfilling this obligation, the Alpha Proposal is offered. Whatever course we choose to take, we must do so with a sense of urgency. Unlike any past generation, ours has the power to stop the process of human history, to kill the Phoenix, by unleashing the nuclear arsenals of the superpowers.

Editor's Comments

Unlike the other essayists in this volume, I have argued that progressively slower growth is likely in the future and that this will accentuate the existing trend toward increasing economic inequality unless corrective action is taken. As the problems of pollution and the national debt become more severe, their consequences may negate the stabilizing effects of a USOP, tearing the social fabric and destroying our economic system.

My proposals for coping with this approaching reality—ranging from a 100 per cent inheritance tax to a population stabilization program—are admittedly idealistic. The contest question was taken as license to dream about conceivable solutions to a host of seemingly intractable problems.

The following essay by John Sedlak separates the issues of creating ideological compatibility and economic democracy. He focuses on attaining economic democracy through a Universal Share Ownership Plan with particular emphasis on modifying the concept to include full-employment and elimination of the national debt in its objectives. He expresses other concerns with the Speiser proposal that sharpen the issues surrounding the creation of a viable USOP. (All numbers within parentheses refer to pages from Stuart Speiser's *How to End the Nuclear Nightmare* [Croton-on-Hudson, NY: North River Press, 1984].)

Modified SuperStock, Full Employment and Elimination of the Federal Debt

by John Sedlak

In his book, *How to End the Nuclear Nightmare,* Stuart Speiser has put forth an economics proposal aimed at minimizing East-West antagonism. His proposal is designed to improve the equitableness and vitality of US capitalism in order to reduce its ideological conflict with Soviet communism. Setting aside for the moment the question of whether or not Speiser's SuperStock plan would be helpful in lessening US-USSR enmity, its value in terms of enhancing the economic well-being of American people can be separately considered.

Speiser's proposal calls for wide distribution of the ownership of the means of production (MOP) in the US and is described in the first chapter of this book. The intended result of the plan is that every American household would, after 20 years, become a capitalist with a $100,000 portfolio of diversified premium (but non-voting and non-transferrable) stock, producing an annual dividend income of about $20,000. The cost of the program would be defrayed by the newly produced wealth, accruing from the corporate investment in new plants and equipment, which would be paid out as dividends.

Aside from East-West political considerations, the main *raison d'être* for a plan like SuperStock is, according to Speiser, the need to overcome increasing economic stagnation and inequity likely to plague the US economy because of growing automation, decreasing opportunities for decent paying jobs and slower rates of growth. With production levels being maintained through automation with much lower levels of manpower, employment will be reduced along with the income distribution that goes with it. As the segment of society that shares in the rewards of owning the MOP shrinks, the entire economy could suffer. Labor and entrepreneurs both would feel the adverse effects of not having a market of people able to afford their products and services. Even programs of employee-ownership would not solve the problem since the beneficiaries of such plans are limited to the limited proportion of the labor force working for well-established, successful corporations, preferably with public traded stock.

By making every American household a substantial MOP owner, SuperStock would assure that the income and wealth generated from the MOP would be broadly distributed, even under conditions of increasing unemployment due to the widespread introduction of robotics. This, according to Speiser, would keep the economy alive and well. A domestic market for products and services would be maintained, thus fueling the engine of enterprise and possibly providing more jobs than might otherwise exist. At the very least, those unemployed and those who would otherwise not receive benefits from ownership of the MOP would be financially supported.

Jobs, Work and SuperStock

Capitalism's potential dilemma arising from growing automation and other trends that reduce decent-paying jobs is likely going to require treatment along the lines of the SuperStock concept of universal MOP ownership. However, in its present form as presented by Speiser, SuperStock would seem to have several significant weaknesses which need to be addressed. The first and most important is that it does not take into account the value of work beyond financial remuneration, and it might reduce the incentive to work with adverse social consequences.

It should be plain that work has a value that goes beyond distributing the income and wealth generated by ownership of the MOP. Society depends on and benefits from the products and services of human labor, and workers gain in self-discipline and self-esteem from productive participation in society. Barbara Blumberg addresses this last point in her book, *The New Deal and the Unemployed,* which focuses on the effects of the 1935-1943 Works Progress Administration (WPA) in New York City. She describes the apparent lift in personal dignity shown by people about to trade their welfare status for a WPA public service job:

> On the most elementary level, these government jobs allowed their holders to survive until private enterprise could again absorb their labor.... But creating work that attempted to utilize the individual's skills and training did much more for him than fill his stomach and provide shelter.... Anzia Yezierska, who was on the Writers' Project in New York, recalled the reaction she and her friends had when they first heard about the emergency work program: "People who no longer hoped or believed in anything but the end of the world began to hope and believe again." As she queued up with others to be interviewed for WPA placement, she noticed the changed manner of her companions. "I had seen these people at the relief station, waiting for the investigation machine to legalize them as paupers. Now they had work cards in their hands. Their waiting was no longer the hopeless stupor of applicants for mass relief; they were employees of the government. They had risen from the scrap heap of the unemployed, from the loneliness of the unwanted.... The new job look lighted the most ravaged faces.[36]

From a religious-moral perspective, it can be added that human work is, by God's design, a sharing in His creative activity and, therefore, is integral to man's nature and well-being. From this would come the conclusion that along with other such economic rights as adequate food, housing and health care, human beings also have a need and a right to work.

Such a view has been embraced by several Catholic leaders. Employment as a requirement of justice, and work as a sharing in the creative activity of God, have been articulated by Pope John Paul II in his 1981 encyclical, *Laborem Excerens (On Human Work)*.[37] The Catholic Bishops of the US have stated that employment is a basic right in the second draft of their pastoral letter, "Catholic Social Teaching and the U.S. Economy."[38]

Speiser acknowledges that wages are the ideal method of supporting people (115) and, as noted earlier, he suggests that SuperStock offers the best hope of preventing mass unemployment by providing that the wealth produced from the MOP would flow as diversified purchasing power into the marketplace, creating a steady demand for goods and services. At the same time, however, he holds that "in an increasingly automated age, no plan is capable of producing full employment"(215) and no government can create enough jobs to support everyone through wages (115). When the robots come, according to Speiser, there will be less and less work available, and in order to give as many people as possible a share in it, "the four day week, and then the three day week, will become the norm, and people will retire at earlier ages" (216). Speiser envisions that with SuperStock providing financial support, the unemployed (and less than fully employed) will constitute a kind of leisure class able to contribute to society via volunteer work in such areas as, for example, environmental protection and social service (217), which might not otherwise get the necessary attention.

In contrast to this rather optimistic view, it can be argued that in a situation of high unemployment the least skilled and capable of enterprise or volunteer humanitarian effort, and perhaps the most in need of productive participation in society through regular employment, would comprise the majority of the new unemployed-leisure group envisioned by Speiser. If this were to be the case, it could be an unhealthy situation for both the individual and society. With less incentive for people to acquire a job skill or to be good providers, one could reasonably be concerned that unemployed-leisure might lend itself as readily to destabilizing social behavior as to productive-creative activity. Opportunity and incentive to work would seem to embody incentive to other behaviors that society values, but if there is decreasing employment opportunity, there will be decreasing incentive to work. And with reduced work incentive, one can expect reduced incentive to other societal values tied to work, such as familial and social stability and productive-creative participation in society requiring self-discipline and providing self-esteem for the individual.

It is widely recognized that work is both necessary for society and valuable to the individual beyond its financial remuneration. Speiser argues that in an increasingly automated era neither business nor government can provide enough jobs for all who are able and willing to work. If this is so, there are compelling reasons for modifying SuperStock to include full employment opportunity in its objectives.

In agreement with Speiser one might concede that in an increasingly automated age business alone will not be able to provide enough jobs for all who are able and want to work. This is not to say that business-generated full employment is inconceivable. One might imagine an ideal world in which many businesses exist primarily to keep people working and living comfortably, if not luxuriously—that is, where enterprise and profit are put at the service of employment and livable wages. But in the real world this is not a likely occurrence since current business economics emphasizes efficiency to maximize profits, and efficiency is perhaps still short-sightedly seen as getting the most production for the least cost, most of which is usually wages.

On the other hand, it is not at all clear that in capitalistic America government cannot create enough jobs to provide gainful work for every citizen able and desirous of working but unable to find livable employment in the private sector. This contention of Speiser's is based primarily on the supposedly high cost of government-created jobs. In this regard he notes that "even back in 1976, it required $50,000 of federal money to create one job paying $8,000 a year" and that under such a government program, "after three years only one or two new jobs remained out of ten supposedly created" (118).

In rebuttal to Speiser's allegation that such jobs cost too much, it can be argued that an $8,000 a year job might, in fact, be worth $50,000 to society. Some of those $8,000 in wages would come back to the government by way of taxes. Most or all of the remainder would be translated into purchasing power that is injected back into the economy, and any portion of the $50,000 cost that is applied to support material or personnel would have the same effect of fueling the economy. On top of all this, there is the value of intangible benefits such as workers' self-discipline and self-esteem accruing from productive participation in the life of society.

If the government cost of supporting an unemployed person through welfare or unemployment compensation, and the potential savings from less crime and smaller taxpayer cost in the treatment of less alcoholism or other psychological or social problems associated with unemployment were subtracted, a $50,000 price tag for an $8,000-a-year government-created job might not be exorbitant. In fact, the Congressional Budget Office has estimated ". . . that in 1986, for every one percentage-point increase in the rate of unemployment, there will be roughly a $40 billion increase in the federal deficit."[39] And that comes to $35,000 per year for each unemployed person. While this figure largely represents revenue losses due to an economy which cannot sustain jobs, it also includes some government outlay to support the unemployed and would reflect the interdependence of work per se and the ancillary jobs and revenue which it can generate and sustain.

All these things considered, it is reasonable to figure that the net cost of government-created jobs could be minimal or even nil. Some government job programs might even turn a small profit and/or be turned into worker-owned or otherwise private enterprises. But even the gross cost of a government-created job is not likely to be as high as $50,000 per year. Early on, the WPA, which paid subsistence wages, operated at an average cost per job of less than 1.5 times its monthly wage rate.[40] Today, under a permanent government jobs program utilizing modern administrative and work management methods, a total cost per job of about 2.5 times its annual wage/benefit rate might reasonably be estimated for the overall program. This would mean that a $10,000 a year government-created jobs, including benefits, would cost about $25,000.

As for the types of jobs that could be created, the possibilities are abundant. From the accomplishments of the WPA, one can get an idea of the range of work projects that were historically possible. A random selection of a small fraction of WPA accomplishments during its first two years is offered by Basil Rauch in his *The History of the New Deal:*

> . . . 1,634 new school buildings, 105 airport landing fields, 3,000 tennis courts, 3,300 storage dams, 103 golf courses, 5,800 traveling libraries established, 1,654 medical and dental clinics established, 36,000 miles of new rural roads, 128,000,000 school lunches served, 2,000,000 home visits by nurses, 1,500 theatrical productions, 134 fish hatcheries, 1,100,000 Braille pages transcribed, and 17,000 literacy classes conducted per month.[41]

Rauch further points out: "The great majority of WPA workers were unskilled laborers, but projects were organized whenever possible to use skilled and professional workers in activities for which they have been trained."[42]

Today, government-created jobs might include, to name just a few examples: (1) the construction and maintenance of public housing; (2)

low-cost home repair for low-income families; (3) additional maintenance of public parks, roads and bridges, as well as for subway and
rail lines and depots; (4) services not otherwise provided to homebound
or handicapped persons; (5) environmental reclamation, beautification
and protection; (6) humanitarian services to developing countries; (7)
supplemental federal, state and local civil service; and (8) operation of
some manufacturing plants or other businesses or utilities in the public
interest.

In general, products and services derived from government-created
work should not and need not compete with or supplant the products
and services provided through existing private sector jobs, unless it is
clearly in the public interest. In some cases public interest might be
determined by a comparison of quality and cost. If, for example, the
quality were higher *and* the cost were lower for certain of the products
and services from government job programs *vis a vis* comparable
products and services from private enterprise, public interest would be
considered best served by maintaining such jobs, even if they supplant
some private sector jobs. The agency responsible for administering job
programs would conceivably have its own research and development
department, supplemented with government-created job workers, to
apply creative thought and energy to the task of generating useful and
efficient government-created jobs and to monitor and rectify government-created job situations causing adverse effects on the private sector. (A separate agency might also be given the task of monitoring the
impact of government-created jobs on private sector jobs. This would
insure an objective appraisal of the situation.)

It would be necessary, of course, that the wages and benefits of
government-created jobs not result in any undue syphoning off of labor
from the private sector. Wage/benefit packages reflecting a minimum
standard for livability would be expected. Hourly wage rates for unskilled work could probably start at the prevailing minimum wage;
skilled and professional work would command higher pay. Step increases in pay based on years of service would be appropriate, and
provisions for shift differential—as well as bonus pay and free-time incentives based on productivity—would be highly desirable. Qualifications and total work seniority from both private jobs and
government-created jobs could determine job placement based on individual preference. Health benefits to workers on government-created
jobs should be at least comparable to those afforded to welfare clients.
Annual wage/benefit packages might realistically start at $10,000 and
have a maximum of $20,000.

While some minimal competition could arise between low-paying private sector work and government job programs, it need not be an unhealthy situation. On the contrary, by establishing minimum standards for livable employment, private enterprise would be challenged to do the same, unless in some cases it chose to rely on part-time workers desiring to supplement their government job income. While this could be slightly inflationary, any competition between private sector work and government job programs would probably have an offsetting, anti-inflationary effect.

The view of Professor Russell A. Nixon, who has served as co-chairman of the National Conference on Public Service Employment, provides a good rebuttal against Speiser's contention that government creation of jobs is unfeasible:

> From the standpoint of current interests and issues, the experience of the 1930s with job creation suggests four major conclusions:
>
> (1) It is feasible for the government, through direct job creating intervention, to create large-scale employment and to cut unemployment extensively.
>
> (2) The productive results of direct government job creation are impressive and socially are dramatically useful.
>
> (3) The job programs of the 1930s were primitive by today's standards. They did not include systematic or significant on-the-job or off-the-job training, had no program of employability creating remedial or support services and included nothing at all in the direction of career development, upgrading or upward mobility.
>
> (4) Expansion of the job-creation programs was successfully opposed by established political powers at all stages so that those programs "fell far short of utilizing as fully as possible the idle economic resources at hand."[43]

Other Concerns with SuperStock

To the primary concern about the value and need for full work opportunity under SuperStock can be added several lesser concerns about Speiser's proposal in its present form. These are: (1) its lack of precise definition regarding stock allocation, (2) its less than optimum method of stock appropriation and (3) the inadequacy of incentives for its international proliferation.

Although Speiser provides some broad specifications regarding allocation of SuperStock portfolios, they are too vague to allow for an analysis of SuperStock's feasibility. On the one hand, Speiser designates the "50 million households who own little or no capital" (132) as the recipients of SuperStock portfolios. On the other hand, he also recognizes that "there would have to be provisions for divorce or breakup of the household" (141). If this means that single adults, divorced or unmarried, would constitute households for the purpose of receiving SuperStock, then the number of eligible households would be substantially greater than 50 million, and the financial requirements might well exceed the proposed $5 trillion in SuperStock appropriations. A modified SuperStock proposal will have to be more precise in specifying the parameters for stock allocation, and individual adults rather than households would seem to be the most workable beneficiary units.

As for SuperStock's method of stock appropriation, it is less than optimum because it would tend to suppress the value of the stock of the participating corporations—to the financial disadvantage of the holders of their non-appropriated stock and to the possible detriment of the corporations themselves. By requiring that all new capital of the participating corporations be paid for by the issuance and appropriation of new, untradeable SuperStock, the value of existing stock would tend to stagnate and perhaps diminish. Without internal or debt financing of the new capital, as the corporate pie increased under SuperStock, that share of the pie represented by existing, non-appropriated stock would decrease, thus suppressing its stock value. While some of this negative effect might be offset by the requirement that participating corporations pay out nearly all of their earnings as dividends, the overall impact on the value of existing stock would seem to be negative.

Speiser is well aware of this situation and the financial disadvantage it would represent for the current stockholders of the corporations participating in SuperStock (219-223), but he does not address its possible adverse consequences for the corporations themselves or for the viability of SuperStock. Suppose, for example, that in an effort to avoid any personal financial disadvantage imposed by SuperStock, the current stockholders of participating corporations decided to break up their corporations, allowing portions of them to be taken over by smaller companies not under the purview of SuperStock legislation. Or suppose the voting stockholders of these corporations decided to relocate their corporation in foreign countries rather than expand under SuperStock, or else to expand only in foreign countries under separate corporate auspices.

Any of these reactions could jeopardize the stability of these leading corporations as well as the viability of SuperStock. A modified SuperStock will have to allow for some potential aggrandizement of the value of a participating corporation's non-appropriated stock by allowing internal or debt financing of some of its new capital. At the same time, in order to minimize the potential for circumventing full participation in SuperStock, the modified plan will also have to be extended to all public stock corporations in the US, and to engage as many foreign countries as possible in adopting comparable programs. Finally, modifying SuperStock so that appropriated stock retains its corporate voting privilege for the holder (but not the government) is recommended because it would seem to offer the advantages of giving Super-Stock portfolio holders a fuller participation in capitalism and of allowing them to exert some influence with regard to corporate commitment to the SuperStock program.

Underlying the concern about the inadequacy of incentives for SuperStock's international proliferation is the larger concern that SuperStock cannot ultimately survive in the US alone. The US needs foreign markets to thrive, and if the dilemma of increasing automation has an impoverishing effect on foreign economies and markets, the US economy will be adversely impacted. Also, without international proliferation of effective SuperStock-like plans, there could be sustained incentives for corporate flight from SuperStock to other countries. And otherwise, with a successful US SuperStock program, there could be an increase in immigration pressures on the US with a potential for overtaxing the US system. A modified SuperStock should therefore include some incentives for its international proliferation, beyond the inherent incentives of its appeal. Open trade arrangements with countries adopting SuperStock-type programs, and restrictive trade arrangements with those countries unwilling to do so, could provide workable incentives for Super Stock's international proliferation.

A Modified SuperStock Plan

Objectives. If we accept universal MOP ownership and full employment opportunity as necessary goals for American capitalism and society in an increasingly automated age, the next step is to examine the feasibility of re-shaping SuperStock to provide for full employment opportunity and to correct the possible weaknesses just described. To this end the following objectives for a modified SuperStock plan are suggested:

(1) To provide gainful employment opportunity for every American citizen 18 to 64 years of age who is able and desirous of working. (Single heads of households with one or more dependents under 18 years of age, and the second parent in two-parent households with one or more such dependents, would not be eligible. Also prisoners along with those duly dismissed from government-created jobs because of discipline problems, would temporarily forfeit their right to work.) Government-created jobs existing for the purpose of providing full employment opportunity should yield an annual wage/benefit package of $10,000 to $20,000 each. These jobs would be financed through a $2.25 trillion stock fund created under modified SuperStock principles. (See Table 1 below for summary cost and population data.)

(2) To provide every work-disabled American citizen 18-64 years of age, with a $60,000 permanent portfolio of non transferrable stock in US-based corporations, providing an expected lifetime annual dividend income of about $12,000.

(3) To provide every American citizen 18 to 64 years of age with an annually incrementing portfolio of non-transferrable stock in US-based corporations. These portfolios should increase in value in approximately equal increments from age 18 until age 64, when the holder can expect to have a $50,000 portfolio providing approximately $10,000 in dividends in a year.

(4) To provide that every American citizen 65 years of age or older has a $50,000 portfolio of non-transferrable stock in US-based corporations, providing an expected annual dividend income of about $10,000.

(5) To promote the proliferation of comparable programs in foreign countries through various incentives, such as open trade policy, with countries which adopt similar programs and restrictive trade policies with those countries which do not.

In addition, by using various combinations of non-allocated dividends from SuperStock and savings from so-called entitlement programs which would be reduced or eliminated through the introduction of SuperStock, it should be possible to pay off the entire federal debt in several decades.

With regard to these objectives, several points should be noted. First of all, the modified SuperStock beneficiaries are individual adults in one of four non-overlapping categories (e.g., a work-disabled person would not be entitled to employment, an incrementing stock portfolio or an additional retirement portfolio). Under this arrangement, a number of federal, state and other programs could be replaced or reduced, including publicly funded disability and retirement programs, unemployment compensation and most current job or job training programs. Public cash assistance programs, such as aid to families with dependent children (A.F.D.C.), would go primarily to single heads of households with at least one dependent under 18 years of age. While it might also be necessary to supplement the income of two-parent households with a large number of children and one parent employed on a government-created job, a substantial reduction in overall A.F.D.C. payments could be expected as a result of the income accruing to households from incremental stock grants and goverrment-created job employment.

Other publicly funded human service programs, including those providing assistance for education, nutrition, housing and health care, would remain intact under this modified arrangement. SuperStock, reshaped according to these modifications, would theoretically achieve the two vitally important goals of full employment opportunity and universal MOP ownership, and would provide minimal support for all US citizens living up to their individual responsibilities. By arranging for the allocation of SuperStock so that individuals, according to a priority system, can select the stock for their portfolios from a pool of available appropriated SuperStock, some of the risks of capitalism would also be retained for those who thus choose to participate in it.

Cost Analysis.   A detailed analysis of SuperStock, modified according to these objectives, would be beyond the scope of this paper. However, a preliminary analysis is included as an appendix to this book, with a brief summation in Table 1 below.

Assuming a constant population and, according to Speiser, a 1:5 stock dividend to stock exchange value ratio (138-140), modified Super Stock would require a total stock fund worth $7.747 trillion. Since this would be largely a revolving fund, no further stock appropriation would be expected, except to expand the program or to maintain the value of the fund as some stocks became defunct. If $150 billion worth of stock could be appropriated annually, it would take about 59 years to accumulate the total stock fund, including a seven-year loan amortization lag (138-140), during which the dividends of the appropriated stock would be applied to the repayment of the government-guaranteed loan for which the stock may have been issued and exchanged.

Table 1

SUMMARY POPULATION AND COST DATA
FOR MODIFIED SUPERSTOCK

(1)   Population Data (in millions of persons):
      a)   total U.S. population...234.0
      b)   under 18 years of age 62.5
      c)   18-64 years of age 144.1
      d)   over 64 years of age...27.4
      e)   work-disabled 18-64 years of age 13.1
      f)   unemployment from private sector and
           seeking work...12.0

(2)   Cost Figures (dividends/stock value at market exchange rate;
      dollar amount in billions [bn] and trillions [tn]):

Value of Stock Portfolios

		Start-Up Cost	Incre-mented Cost	Fully Opera-tional Stock Fund
a)	12 million government-created jobs paying $10-20,000/yr. in wages and benefits at a cost 2.5 times wage/benefit package (annual dividend income, $450 bn).	2.25 tn	0	$2.25 tn
b)	19.7 million stock portfolios each generating approx. $12,000/yr. for persons over 17 yrs. of age, judged to be work-disabled at age 18 to 64 yrs. (annual dividend income, $236.4 bn).	1.182 tn	0	1.182 tn
c)	Annual stock grants each generating approx. $218/yr. for 131 million non-work-disabled persons 18 to 64 yrs. of age (dividend income of $28.6 bn the first year, increased by $6.26 bn annually over 45 years).	143 bn	3.132 tn (over 45 years)	3.275 tn

Table 1 (continued)

d) 20.8 million stock portfolios each generating about $10,000/yr. for persons over 64 yrs. of age not previously work-disabled (annual dividend income, $2.8 bn).	1.04 tn	0	1.04 tn

Various parts of the program, however, could be implemented long before this. Depending on the number of unemployed persons and on how the dividends accruing to the government from the temporary holding of appropriated stock were to be allocated, the government-created jobs portion of the program would be fully operational in the first 22 years or less. In 38 years all work-disabled persons and persons over 64 years of age will have received the complete stock portfolios to which they are entitled. Also, all other citizens ages 18 to 64 will have received their first annual stock portfolio installment valued at about $1,087, and this would then be incremented by an equal amount for each of the next 45 years or until at age 65 the individual becomes entitled to a full $50,000 portfolio.

If all non-allocated dividends accruing to the government from the temporary holding of appropriated stock were applied to paying off a budget-balanced, $3 trillion federal debt principal, it could be eliminated in 21 years. And even if no budget funds were targeted to pay an annual 6.5 per cent interest payment on a $3 trillion federal debt, whose only potential growth was the annual interest payment, the debt could be eliminated in 52 years if all non-allocated dividends accruing to the government from the temporary holding of appropriated stock, and all savings from programs superseded by modified SuperStock, were applied to its interest payment and principal.

And so, while modified SuperStock would not reach full maturity until 83 years of age, four out of five major milestones could be realized by age 59: (1) full employment, (2) universal MOP ownership, (3) elimination of federal debt and (4) acquisition of the total modified SuperStock fund.

If the $7.747 trillion value of the total stock fund is taken as the gross cost of modified SuperStock, its actual or net cost would be this figure minus the savings realized from the discontinuation or diminution of public programs overlapped and superseded by modified Super-Stock. It turns out that during the 83-year span of modified SuperStock's full maturation, at least $11.902 trillion in public human service outlays will have been replaced by modified SuperStock. A net savings of $4.155 trillion from superseded programs would thus be realized during the maturation period of the program. Thereafter, annual savings of about $255 billion a year could be expected as a result of modified SuperStock. It should be noted that these are savings figures from superseded programs only, and they do not include interest savings realized after paying off the federal debt nor the savings realized by applying non-allocated modified SuperStock dividends to other programs after the federal debt has been paid off. Under the scenario of a budget-balanced, $3 trillion debt principal, eliminated in 21 years by the application of non-allocated modified SuperStock dividends, interest savings and unused, non-allocated dividends would total $17.508 trillion at the end of modified SuperStock's maturation period.

Paying for Modified SuperStock. In the long run, as indicated above, modified SuperStock would pay for itself. What needs to be considered, then, is how the program could be financed and who, if anyone, would be the financial losers under it.

Speiser notes that "over the next generation (roughly 20 years), according to the Brookings Institution, *Business Week* and other authoritative sources, new capital expenditures (from American business) are expected to total at least $5 trillion" (129). "In 1982," Speiser points out, "even at a time of crippling recession, American business invested over $300 billion in the construction and purchase of new plants and equipment." (124).

Using these figures, along with Speiser's assertion that a 20 per cent return on invested capital would be realized if all corporate earnings (except for reserves actually needed to run the company) were paid out as dividends, it is clear that modified SuperStock is economically feasible. If one-half of American business' annual new capital investments were financed through appropriated stock, modified SuperStock's total operating fund could, as noted above, be acquired in 59 years, including a seven-year loan amortization lag. This leads to the following recommendations for financing modified SuperStock:

(1) With the initiation of modified SuperStock, every existing US-based public stock corporation will be required to issue (for appropriation by the US agency administering modified SuperStock) new stock in order to finance not less than 50 per cent of its capital improvements or expansions.

(2) New US-based public stock corporations, formed after modified SuperStock has been initiated, will be required to issue (for appropriation by the modified SuperStock administration agency) new stock for not less than 50 per cent of its initial capital investment and later improvements or expansions.

(3) All US-based public stock corporations will be required under modified SuperStock to allocate as dividends all earnings realized from their improvement, expansion or establishment financed by appropriated stock, less that amount needed to operate that portion of the corporation financed by appropriated stock.

(4) Under modified SuperStock, the 2,000 leading US-based public stock corporations, and those others registering a profit of at least $1 million the previous year, will be eligible for government-guaranteed loans in exchange for the appropriated stock issued for capital improvements or expansion; newly established corporations, likewise, will be eligible for government-guaranteed loans in exchange for the appropriated stock issued for their initial capital investment and for later capital improvements or expansion.

(5) Under modified SuperStock, all US-based public stock corporations will be exempt from paying federal, state and local corporate income taxes; these taxes will be retained and stiffened for private companies.

Under these five stipulations, the $4.615 trillion appropriated stock fund needed for the start-up of modified SuperStock could be generated in about 38 years. In another 21 years the total fund could be acquired. Beyond this, appropriated stock in excess of what is projected to be necessary to operate modified SuperStock could allow for program operation in the case of an increasing US population or higher unemployment.

Although Wall Street and current stockholders have already been identified by Speiser as apparent losers under SuperStock (219-223), the aforementioned financing recommendations for modified Super-Stock are intended to minimize any negative impact on these. By requiring corporations to fund only 50 per cent of their capital improvements or expansion by the issuance of new, appropriated stock in exchange for government-guaranteed loans, current stockholders could still expect at least some increase in the value of their stocks (through internal or debt financing of up to 50 per cent of capital improvements).

As for Wall Street's stockbrokers, a substantial reduction in the volume of tradeable stock would seem to affect them negatively. But modified SuperStock's specification that federal, state and local income taxes be abolished for public stock corporations (at the same time retained and stiffened for private companies) could offset some of the loss in tradeable stock volume by inducing some large private companies to "go public."

Finally, the facilitation of capital funding afforded by modified SuperStock to existing and new corporations over the long term (i.e., at least 51 years) could spur the economy so that both Wall Street and current stockholders realize a substantial net gain.

In sum, then, modified SuperStock appears to be feasible and affordable.

The East-West Question

If East-West antagonism was the product of economic ideological differences alone, SuperStock would go a long way toward easing this enmity, and modified SuperStock with its provision for full employment opportunity would go even farther. Unfortunately, the problem seems to be deeper and more subtle than this. While Western democracy and capitalism recognize that government exists for the good of individuals who comprise a society, Eastern communism sees individuals as existing for the common good or the good of the state. This is why, for example, the Soviet Union and other Communist countries refuse free emigration for their citizens. The state sees individuals as belonging to it, particularly if the state has invested in their education. Similarly, this is why free information exchange is not tolerated. Once born, the Communist state seeks its self-preservation even against the will of the vast majority of its citizens who, if exposed to a free exchange of ideas and information, might threaten it.

The incompatibility of statist communism and democratic capitalism lies, then, not so much in differing economic views (i.e., free market vs. centrally planned economies) or in differing political views, as it does in differing views about the relationship of the individual to the state. Influenced by Judaism and Christianity, Western civilization upholds the individual's inherent rights which are seen as endowed by God and not by the state. Born of an atheistic philosophy, communism sees the state as the sole giver of human rights. Therefore, even if a Communist society could adopt some form of capitalism, it is inconceivable that it could ever comfortably tolerate a constitutional democracy which recognizes individual human rights that exist independently of the state. Indeed, the dynamic of atheistic communism would always seem to be toward state control of the individual, wherever he might be. Without some sort of acknowledgment of a loving God, or at least some sort of recognition of individual rights that transcend the state, it is unlikely that communism and democracy of the US variety can peacefully co-exist in the long run.

Modified SuperStock, or even the original SuperStock plan, would seem to represent an advance for capitalism, which may have to be adopted in some form if capitalist economies are to remain vibrant. If successfully nurtured in developing countries, it might even have some value in preventing the spread of communism to those indigent countries which are so desperate for development and social justice that they might otherwise embrace a Communist system which promises these at the expense of individual freedoms. But ultimately, it will take more than SuperStock or modified SuperStock to end the nuclear nightmare.

Editor's Comments

Unlike the editor, who looked at the economy from the point of view of stagnation, Sedlak assumes continuing growth fueled by massive automation. Given that workers lose jobs faster than new ones are created, or if the new jobs acquired entail significantly lower pay, a more rapid and profound increase in income/wealth inequality may ensue. In an environment without a USOP, unemployment will rise and the social welfare establishment will become more pervasive. The existence of a USOP would give the unemployed dividend income to support themselves. But Sedlak cautions that we are not acknowledging the importance of work. We have already noted that Karl Marx argued that one's job, and the nature of that job, is one of the most crucial elements in defining one's being. Sedlak takes a spiritual view of the issue, unlike Marx's materialist view, but comes to the same conclusion. From this he asserts that people have a right, as well as a need, to work. Any proposed change of capitalism must reflect this basic fact.

Speiser claims that a USOP will free individuals to do the "work of humanity" so that unemployment will not pose a problem. Sedlak argues that work centers a person in values conducive to social stability. Take away one's work and they are just as likely to gravitate to socially destructive activities as to the "work of humanity." This was the motivation behind his proposal for "government-created jobs."

Neysa Chouteau makes some illuminating suggestions on modifying SuperStock in her essay, "Toward Realizing the Dream: A Response

to *How to End the Nuclear Nightmare.*" Chouteau also argues that the
USOP concept should be separated from the ideological compatibility
question. Her specific recommendations for modifying SuperStock can
be gleaned from the following excerpt. (All numbers in parentheses
refer to pages in Speiser's book, *How to End the Nuclear Nightmare.*)

Contribution by Neysa Chouteau

First, make SuperStock a mutual fund. The SuperStock
shareholders then own shares of SuperStock rather than having a
situation whereby "in a given year a SuperStockholder might
receive a certificate of ownership for 9 shares of IBM, 12 shares of
General Motors, 6 shares of Exxon, and so on . . ." (134). This
should also eliminate the need for a given corporation to issue "a
special type of stock, to be called SuperStock" (133). The corporation issues regular stock which becomes a part of the SuperStock
mutual fund portfolio. Procedures suggested in Speiser's book
(133-134) would generate enormous amounts of paperwork for
both the corporations and the government agency involved. Creating a SuperStock mutual fund would simplify matters considerably.
Also, if SuperStock is a mutual fund, there need be little concern
about whether or not the shares are non-voting because Super-
Stockholders do not own shares in the corporations involved; they
own shares in the mutual fund only.

Second, plan for implementing SuperStock as quickly as possible.
Speiser suggests two possibilities: that all dividends go to the banks
until the loans are repaid (133-134) or that the repayment period be
stretched out and part of the dividends begin to go to SuperStock
shareholders immediately (140). In order to generate maximum
public enthusiasm, some dividends should begin immediately.

Third, avoid the morass of planning to distribute SuperStock to
"households." Speiser repeatedly speaks of SuperStockholders in
terms of households (134, 141-142). He spotlights some of the difficulty in focusing on households as recipients when he states
"some weight would have to be given to the number of people in
the household, and . . . there would have to be provisions for divorce
or breakup of the household" (141). Keeping track of changing
households or legislating what group of persons constitutes a
household is a problem that SuperStock does not need. Make the
distribution to "persons" rather than to "households."

Fourth, simplify the question of access to SuperStock. Speiser devotes several pages to the question of who the SuperStockholders would be (140-143). He points out that there will be wide differences of opinion, that "liberals will want to give welfare recipients first crack at SuperStock benefits. Conservatives will probably want the benefits to be divided evenly among all registered voters, regardless of present wealth" (143). To avoid the divisive and distracting process of deciding who should get what, distribute Super-Stock shares to *every* citizen who is 21 years old or older, but distribute the shares in inverse proportion to each person's gross income as reported on his or her federal income tax return or sworn to on an affidavit. For example:

$ Gross Income	Shares of SuperStock
0	100
10,000	90
50,000	50
90,000	10
100,000 up	1

SuperStock shares are to be issued in yearly installments to each person 21 years old and older until that person has been issued enough shares to generate $10,000 in dividend income. Persons with large incomes from other sources will receive such a token number of shares each year that they may not live long enough to reach $10,000 in SuperStock income.

Those who are on welfare, social security or other government payment programs would have their government payments reduced each year by 80 per cent of the dividends they receive from Super-Stock, until eventually the dividends exceed the government payments by enough of a margin to eliminate the government payments completely.

For purposes of SuperStock distribution, spouses who file joint income tax returns would be assumed to share that income equally, no matter which spouse earned it. That is, if the couple had a gross income of $20,000, each spouse would be counted as having a gross income of $10,000 for SuperStock purposes and would be issued shares of SuperStock in his or her own name.

Fifth, make corporate participation in SuperStock voluntary. Mr. Speiser envisions that corporations be *required* to finance growth through issuing SuperStock shares and *required* to pay out all their earnings as dividends (129). In keeping with the essay ideal of not "giving up our treasured freedoms," corporate participation should be voluntary and the SuperStock plan for raising new capital should be so attractive that corporations will be eager to participate. Speiser's plan envisions the mechanisms through which this could be achieved—primarily through offering interest rates that are low enough to be more attractive than other loan sources (140), and through changes in the corporate income tax structure (139). Speiser suggests that the corporate income tax could be lifted for SuperStock dividends through tax deductions. This move could be made sweeter by allowing the corporations a matching tax deduction for regular (non-SuperStock) dividends. Thus, for every share of SuperStock a corporation generated, it would get tax relief on two shares, the SuperStock share and a regular share.[44]

Later in her essay, Chouteau echoes Sedlak by observing that Speiser's plan contains no mechanism for worldwide proliferation of the concept. She states that the goal of reducing nuclear tensions and achieving diplomatic breakthroughs should not be forgotten. Provision should be made, she argues, for "reserving a small percentage of Super-Stock dividends for SuperStock International; an agency that would use its SuperStock funds to offer partnership proposals, technical advice and possibly loans to other countries who are interested in implementing SuperStock or SuperStock-inspired plans in their own countries. In other words, the SuperStock International agency would explore and implement many of the suggestions on pages 170 to 185 of Speiser's book, such as developing joint projects with the Soviets, helping establish SuperStock enterprises in Third World countries, and offering information or suggestions for joint ventures to any industrialized nations that request it."[45]

James Albus also takes issue with Speiser's proposal to make corporate participation mandatory. In his essay, "An Industrial Policy That Would Work . . . for Everyone," he argues that forcing firms to belong to the USOP is not politically feasible.

Contribution by James Albus

SuperStock makes a major contribution to the concept of Universal Capitalism by extending the availability of stock ownership to the entire population. The principal defect in the SuperStock proposal is that it would require legislation forcing the nation's 2,000 largest firms to participate (i.e., to forego all future capital financing methods except for SuperStock financing). This degree of coercion is probably not politically acceptable in the present climate.

Peoples' Capitalism is an economic proposal formulated by the author in 1976.[46] It would give everyone an ownership stake in wealth-producing capital stock through a National Mutual Fund (NMF). The NMF would use credits from the Federal Reserve Bank to make new investments in private industries through purely voluntary agreements, and would pay dividends on those investments to the public on an equal per capita basis. . . . Each adult citizen would effectively own one share of non-negotiable stock in the National Mutual Fund.

The National Mutual Fund would invest in private industrial firms using an investment strategy designed to maximize return on investment. The invested funds would be used by private industry to build new plants and purchase new production equipment. A negotiated percentage of the profits from these investments would be paid back to the National Mutual Fund which would distribute dividends on earnings to the public.[47]

This short excerpt does not do justice to Albus' considerable effort at formulating an alternative to a USOP. What it does point out is the fact that a USOP could be restructured to make voluntary participation attractive. If the National Mutual Fund purchased debt and equity instruments in the private sector and paid out returns to all American citizens, it would be functionally identical to a USOP. Beyond the compulsory participation issue, the Speiser and Albus models differ in that the National Mutual Fund would represent a de facto national industrial policy. This is not a bad feature in itself, but it opens up an entirely new area for discussion.

Several authors questioned Speiser's implicit claim that a USOP should be established on the national level. This particular contingent of essayists drew on the work of E. F. Schumacher *(Small is Beautiful)*, Kirkpatrick Sale *(Human Scale)*, Paul Hawken *(The Next Economy)*, Alvin Toffler *(The Third Wave)* as well as others from this school of thought. Their vision of a new society, which embodies the values of economic democracy and peace, would be centered in politics and economies that assure control by the people. Donald Clark's paper, "Devolution: A Path to Stable Peace" is a good example of this genre of essayist. In the spirit of the authors mentioned above Clark argues that society needs to be restructured for a more stable, human balance between the existing centers of power and what he terms the "periphery." The periphery consists of those individuals and regional organizations that have been disenfranchised within the democratic and economic processes. The term "devolution" is used by Clark to mean an outward flow of decision-making authority from the power centers to the periphery.

Contribution by Donald Clark

In developing a coherent devolutionist policy for the United States the principal actor must be the economic sector, appropriately reversing the process by which supralocal connections were first created. The objective of this policy will be the development of cohesive, functional and economically viable regions, autonomous but politically and economically interdependent. The following program will allow devolutionary America to emerge as a progressive member of the family of nations.

The crucial first step is to bring about a transformation in the management, ownership and organizational patterns of major corporations. This transformation of American corporations has three dimensions, each of which is necessary in forging a devolutionary society.

The first, *participatory management,* is already the subject of significant attention and debate. The reason is simple; the corporation is one of the institutions from which consent is being withdrawn, and employees no longer recognize a bond of unquestioning commitment. Bound by financial necessity, they will still work with varying degrees of inefficiency in non-participatory situations. But full engagement, creativity, enthusiasm and selflessness occur in a participatory atmosphere in which the employee knows himself to be an organic, power-sharing part of the company. It is for this reason that the transformation of management is well into the experimental stage with theory struggling to catch up with practice.

The issues surrounding the second aspect of corporate transformation, *universal ownership* of America's major productive assets, are best stated by Stuart Speiser in *How to End the Nuclear Nightmare.*

In his proposal the new capital needed by America's 2,000 largest corporations, estimated at about $300 billion per annum, is the key to devolving ownership. SuperStock shareholders, however, would not be able to vote their shares, a reservation which, in relation to large centralized corporations, is justifiable and does not constitute a major objection to the plan.

It does, however, indicate the need for a third kind of corporate transformation, *regional organization*. The devolutionary corporation will be organized not by national divisions based on product lines, but by geography with the locus of integration at the regional level. This corporate "federalization" dovetails with universalization of ownership by turning the corporation into a coordinated network of interdependent sub-companies each of which is majority-owned and *controlled* by the people of the market area which it serves.

Economists must soon develop a sound understanding of the process of corporate devolution and detail the advantages which lie along this path. There are many and, as the new vision matures, the pace of change will be reinforced by positive feedback from both employees and customers.[48]

This passage suggests Clark's support for both universal capital ownership and worker self-managed enterprises. The major contribution which he makes is to cast both models in the light of a more general process of social change. He sees both models as effective means to redistribute income, ownership and, more fundamentally, decision-making power during the near-term future. This is the heart of the "participatory democracy" philosophy which Clark adheres to.

Clark goes on to argue that regional enterprises should be built on the foundation of cooperation and service rather than competition and profit maximization. The final component of his thesis is focused on public support for and education in the precepts of participatory planning and cooperative action. While important in the overall context of the process he describes, these subsequent steps are only marginally germane to the subject of this chapter and will not be more fully discussed here.

Another approach to decentralizing societal power in the context of a USOP is proposed by Cheryl Dickerson in her essay, "Methods of Harmonizing American Capitalism and Marxism in a Unified Effort to Prevent a Nuclear Holocaust." Her proposals are along "States' Rights" lines and focus on decentralizing the administrative structure of a USOP. In her plan the federal government would pass the required legislation, provide temporary financing for the participating corporations and collect the USOP shares. These shares would then be distributed to the states, which in turn distribute them to the county level. A special long-term loan program will be structured into the USOP legislation and comes into play here. The county government working with local financial institutions will arrange the issuance of a long-term loan in the names of all local citizens for the financing of issued USOP shares. It is not clear from Dickerson's essay, but apparently the federal government will either provide some part of the money for the loan or at least guarantee the loan. However this last point is to be handled, the USOP shares will be held in escrow by the local financial institutions until the dividends paid liquidate the entire loan.

Once the loans are liquidated, the local citizens will be transferred title on their portion of the USOP shares and receive all future dividends. There are more details to her proposal, yet those mentioned outline its basic form. Her plan would greatly decentralize the administrative aspect of a USOP by involving all levels of government. Dickerson seems to suggest that in many instances USOP shares issued could be for local businesses. This means that people will eventually own incorporated businesses in their region. A USOP would become more community-oriented under this plan with strong incentives for USOP shareholders to become more active in participating in the affairs of their local firms.

Given the obvious ambiguities in the Constitution, Kevin Ketchum argues in his essay, "Expanding the Democratic Ideal: A Redefinition of Free Enterprise," that we may need a constitutional amendment recognizing an individual's right to economic opportunity. The arguments for such an amendment are basically the same as those for the Equal Rights Amendment for women.

Contribution by Kevin Ketchum

To achieve completely equitable distribution, we must first be willing to recognize formally a distributive right, a positive claim of each citizen upon our societal resources protected by the force of law. This might require a constitutional amendment. The United States once refused to accept a United Nations proposal to recognize economic rights because they were perceived at the time to go far beyond the rights contained in the United States Constitution. Franklin Roosevelt spoke of an economic bill of rights, but they were not realized as part of the New Deal due to a shift to conservatism which left us with our current system of welfare capitalism. But by whatever formal process—Constitutional amendment, legislative enactment or judicial interpretation—we, as a nation, must finally bring our economic agenda in line with our social agenda.

Socially, we encourage pluralism, a respect for individual choice. However, because the prevailing view in our country is that the market is the embodiment of individual free choice, such choice only has meaning if one has the economic means to make his choice a reality. Justice Felix Frankfurter once said that "the history of liberty has largely been the history of procedural safeguards." The most profound result of this history has been to insure that what we possess as the means to pursue happiness in life will not be arbitrarily taken away. But this concept of liberty should not be a license to sustain inequity. Rather, equity should be vital to our concept of liberty so that more of our fellow citizens can obtain that which our procedural safeguards allow us to keep.

A recognition of distributive rights is, of course, a recognition that a truly free man is one who can look forward to tomorrow with the confidence that he will not suddenly be deprived of the means of subsistence. But we should not be satisfied with meeting subsistence needs. We should seek to provide a "decent standard of living" for everyone. By doing so we can provide a real foundation for the enjoyment by all of formally recognized political and personal rights, and thus truly accomplish the democratic ideal.

Once distributive rights are recognized, they can be given substance by practical reforms which will draw upon the strengths of our capitalist economic system and will modify or discard those practices which create inequities that are in conflict with our democratic ideal.[49]

Later in his essay, in discussing the SuperStock model Ketchum suggests:

It might be desirable for everyone to "earn" SuperStock benefits by contributing to society in some tangible, measurable way. For instance, those already employed might be called upon to participate in community service work in addition to their full-time job in order to be eligible for benefits. The unemployed might be required to work for agencies similar to the Works Progress Administration and others created in the 1930s New Deal program. Such agencies would provide a mechanism for the government to plan and achieve activities in the public interest without forcing public interest planning on America's corporations.[50]

Ketchum also fears that the Speiser's SuperStock proposal would be destructive to the work ethic. Some type of mechanism must be structured into the plan providing incentives to work. It would be much more desirable if these incentives were positive rather than negative in nature. This would reduce USOP shareholders' efforts to avoid work and enhance the social stabilizing effects of a USOP.

Finally, Ketchum feels strongly that:

> For a plan like SuperStock to succeed in achieving universal capitalism and, therefore, greater economic equity, we must create an environment which will encourage the positive aspect of capitalism—investment in new capital to increase production of goods. Unfortunately, recent years have witnessed policies that have favored finance over enterprise.
>
> Low taxation of capital gains, direct control of the money supply by monetary authorities and loans to support margin trading on the stock exchanges all encourage speculation—the rearrangement of existing wealth—while diverting money from enterprise—the investment in new capital. Speculation not only diverts money from enterprise, but also, by depending on rising prices, is itself a stimulant to further price rises.
>
> It is time to reverse these trends and return to true enterprise by encouraging investment in new capital. To do this we must reverse policies that encourage speculation which takes the form of investment in existing wealth at the expense of enterprise. Also, it may be necessary again to regulate banking to decrease competition and provide a climate for the reduction of interest rates.[51]

Ketchum is not the only author who feels that the social, economic and political environment in which the USOP operates is crucial. The editor argued in his essay earlier in this chapter that there are factors which may undermine the integrity of a program of expanded capital ownership, such as the national debt and population growth. Francis Kingen's argument for reforming the world monetary system was introduced in Chapter II. Florian Zaleweski's essay, which was cited in Chapter III, is again quoted here because it addresses the same environmental concern.

Capital ownership distribution will be hindered without the reorganization of money and banking. Economics involves the study of indirect exchange, that is, a study of human action in which the transactions are mediated with the use of money. Therefore, a clearly defined monetary unit is a crucial element in all efforts to distribute capital ownership worldwide and will require a thorough reorganization of the banking system.[52]

The important point here is that a USOP, or some other plan such as Wisman's for worker ownership, is a necessary but insufficient condition for reaching the goal of economic democracy. The political, cultural, economic and international context of such a plan can nurture or undermine the effectiveness of the program in attaining the desired goal. To be blind to these forces is foolish. To begin a dialogue on the relationship between the social environment and any plan to reform American capitalism is to pave the way to a final proposal which will be effective as well as robust.

Americans find it easy to dismiss the international arena. It has already been mentioned that many essayists feared that the SuperStock plan was flawed since it was built upon an implicit sense of American superiority. The model does not embody a mechanism for international participation. Once again, America acts and the world is expected to follow. Francisco Muller's essay, "From the Nuclear Nightmare to the American Dream," was primarily concerned with this issue.

Contribution by Francisco Muller

SuperStock requires a humanistic re-education of the entire American citizenship. It is too precious a thing, too radical a change to imagine that its effects will automatically follow as with an ordinary taxation law. Why? I do not think one has to be a genius on the economy to predict that an entire nation of capitalists, in the selfish and materially self-expansive sense of the term, each one trying to acquire and consume more and more things, (especially the type of unnecessary wants so abundant in consumerist societies), will improve at all the situation of the Third World. While more equality may be achieved among Americans, a greater inequality will result with the rest of the world, especially the Third World.

Only through extensive re-education would Americans become globally conscious and morally responsible for all the poor of the world and translate this into an effective action of self-control (as they sing in "America the Beautiful"), so that the economy is directed toward meeting true needs and not luxury wants. Ultimately, they must come to realize that world peace is at stake here and that as "needless wants" multiply, more gasoline is thrown into the fire of international envy, revenge and aggression which can finally ignite the nuclear cataclysm. As C. F. von Weizsacker so aptly observes, the problem, the big problem, is that everybody wants peace but they do exactly the opposite of what is required to obtain it.

SuperStock, therefore, ought to be designed and calculated in its effect upon the whole world, the Soviet Union included, even if initially only the US can adopt such a policy. Universal capitalism must be truly universal, at least in spirit and in theory. Anything short of this will cause it to fail in the long run.

In recognition of this supremacy of politics over the economy, the SuperStock program ought to be presented and in the spirit of consultation with the Soviet Union. Only then might it elicit the desired peaceful and friendly effect. Just like a marriage between two individuals, a "marriage" among nations can only be proposed, never imposed. Imposition is the ugly face of aggression. Proposition is the joyful spirit of friendliness and generosity.

What if after all this, the Soviet Union still distrusts and criticizes all our moves? We can still "disengage unilaterally," as Speiser says, because we will be acting independently but not selfishly. If Super-Stock is launched under the banner of justice, supported by the necessary re-education of its beneficiaries and with a view to entire world needs, then we would have acquired something more than power, something more than weapons and money—a new moral strength, a new authority based in that strength.[53]

Muller and other essayists suggest that instituting a plan for universal and equitable capital ownership, based squarely on the principle of economic democracy, will provide a historically unprecedented opportunity for American foreign policy. The demonstrable moral and ethical superiority of a USOP will permit our government to transform the meaning of America as a global power promoting world peace.

VII.

A SEARCH FOR SOLUTIONS

Every gun that is made, every warship launched, every rocket fired
signifies, in the final sense, a theft from those who hunger and are not
fed, those who are cold and are not clothed. This world in arms is not
spending money alone; it is spending the sweat of its laborers, the
genius of its scientists, the hope of its children.

—Dwight D. Eisenhower

Editor's Introduction

The preceding chapter led back to the issue of world peace, although this time the path followed was American economic reform
rather than ideological convergence. The two paths share a common
destination, but there are significant differences. Whereas the question
of ideology revolves around social consciousness, the issue of
economic reform involves the social structures defining established arrangements for production and distribution of goods, services, income
and wealth. While one is concerned with the mind of society, the other
is concerned with the body. They both form an interactive, interdependent, inseparable whole.

If we wish to enhance economic democracy in the US, establishing
a plan for universal capital ownership will move us in the right direction. The extent, character and feasibility of economic reform are important issues addressed by the essayists included in earlier chapters.

There are many factors in the social and natural environment which could undermine a USOP's effectiveness. Depending on those other factors a USOP could be highly successful or a meaningless sham. Essayists proposed ancillary institutional changes that would either mitigate these other factors or extend the scope of economic justice.

When the issue of ideological convergence is introduced, the discussion becomes even more complex. The goals of ideological convergence, economic justice and world peace are indeed interrelated, but the nature of that interrelationship is elusive. We have learned that national and global problems weave together in unexpected ways. A solution to one problem (e.g., economic injustice) must take into account many other related problems (e.g., pollution, national debt, the North-South question and so forth). This last perception was best articulated in Larry Marshall's essay, "Synergistic Solutions: A Tapestry of Great Power."[1] These extended excerpts from that essay identify critical barriers to be overcome in the quest for a workable and sustainable solution to American economic injustice and the nuclear nightmare.

Synergistic Solutions:
A Tapestry of Great Power
by Larry Marshall

Wealth and Power

Both the United States and the Soviet Union are now struggling with stagnating economies. Both have huge problems with pollution (as does the whole industrial world). Powerful, entrenched and debilitatingly large bureaucracies and vested economic and political interests constipate both. Both find their once seemingly inexhaustible resources dangerously limited. Both continue to squander their economic might on military protection of access to raw materials and markets throughout the world. And as Jonathan Kwitny observes in *Endless Enemies,* both nations have governments which find it very convenient to have enemies with ideologies antagonistic to their own.[2]

I submit that all of these problems point to a common industrial-economic malady. We need to transcend this industrial/us-against-nature/reductionistic paradigm, not fix it. By itself, SuperStock is an attempt to fix it. Integrated with other solutions, it could be part of a transcending strategy—the emergence of a new trans-capital, trans-Communist, trans-industrial synthesis.

The fundamental difference between capitalism and communism is in their approaches to private wealth. Capitalists protect private wealth. Communists attack it. Both are wrong answers to the right question: Why do we not *all* have enough?

Capitalism seems more efficient, but in its extreme leads to abuses through emphasizing the rights of individuals over those of society as a whole. The power that accumulates to the successful economic entity becomes so great as to allow a virtual dictatorship of the status quo. Peter Navarro has concluded in *The Policy Game: How Special Interests and Ideologies Are Stealing America* that as vested interests apply their dominant power to preventing essential changes, they stop the evolution of a vital society.[3]

Marx foresaw and forewarned us of this. He also suggested a way out. As the exploitation of the working class by the capital class became unbearably disproportionate, the oppressed would overthrow the tyrants. The working class is the only social agent of a power capable of counteracting the great political/economic power of capital wealth. After the revolution, return on capital would be distributed among all citizens through the mechanism of socialized ownership of the means of production. Thus, a fundamental premise of communism is redistribution of wealth.

Politically, the essence of wealth is power. Wealth buys public opinion, especially through today's media. Its effects are pervasive. Money is the lifeblood of industrial society. The extent and insidious corrosiveness of its power was the essence of Marx's sociological insight. Initially, I felt that SuperStock's overt attack upon wealth in a capitalistic society spelled its political doom. Now I am not so sure.

On first view, Speiser's idea seems merely to dress the same old Marxist dogma of socializing the means of production with a new cloak of respectability. Its weakness appears to lie within the veiled, but still too apparent, attack upon wealth and upon the wealthy's continued access to new wealth. It seems to be an attack against one of the most critical needs of the wealthy to preserve their access to the position of comfort and power. This is not a thing of intellect. It is a thing of emotion—primitive emotion. SuperStock attacks a core concept of being wealthy—becoming more wealthy.

Speiser's appropriation of capital formation is a threat to the continuation of the power structure of capital society today. Should public interest in SuperStock start to roll, the powers that be would strive to bring about SuperStock's doom. However, if we are to move to the abundant age that our technological creativity promises, the wealthy must, *in self-defense,* learn to share access to new wealth in society. That is Speiser's insight! Is it possible? Only if the left understands that private ownership is not the only cause of our problems. Only if the right understands that totally unfettered access to wealth is ultimately self-defeating. And only if both the left and the right agree that political change through violence was made obsolete by nuclear weapons.

Revolution today must transcend violence. We need a process through which we can create revolutionary change without resorting to the dialectical ploy of waiting for the proletariat to get so fed up that they violently "throw the rascals out." This is also what Speiser is suggesting. We must achieve such an overwhelming consensus of political vision that the established structures of power become convinced that this unfolding future image is essential to their own security.

To achieve this consensus such changes might be cloaked in short-term monetary gain. An essential political insight is the typical narrowness of view of our Trolls, those who measure "good" through the blinders of next year's profits. Getting them to overlook possible long-term losses might well be done by waving large near-term gains in front of their noses.

Technology, Affluence and Resource

Realistic non-violent strategies for change must relate to both ideologies, their self-images, strengths and weaknesses. Speiser is suggesting SuperStock as a way of guaranteeing the social needs of society without nationalizing wealth. But is maldistribution of wealth within a nation the real problem of the world? And will a more fair distribution of wealth within a society resolve the arms race, or any other of the world's overwhelming problems? I think not, at least not alone as an independent strategy.

A key fact in the current world situation is that technology has brought unparalleled affluence to the first and second worlds. All economically successful nations are, at this point in history, industrial nations which have eagerly applied the tools that science and industry have afforded them. Both dominant political/economic models rest on essentially technological/industrial economies, only differing in details.

In reality, communism is also an economy built on capital. It is just that its capital, its means of production, is controlled by the elite of the state rather than by the market and the economic elite of private wealth. Although communal ownership may indeed, at least in theory, be more "moral" than private ownership, it is nonetheless stuck with the same

roadblock to self-transcendence as capitalism. It creates a power structure with strong interests in maintaining power—and thus avoiding
change. Increased affluence for its people flows from exponential
growth in the exploitation of the natural world. It is as dependent as
capitalism on the retention of a percentage of its surplus as reinvest-
ment capital to improve processing of raw material in the pursuit of
growth. As much as in any capitalistic state, Communist success is indicated by a "quality of life," as measured by material consumption.

Access to resources is vital, according to Daniel Yergin and Martin Hillenbrand.[4] The pride of industrial society rests in its ability to exploit the natural resources of this planet. Both capitalism and
communism have been successful in using technology to turn natural
resources into human goods for all their people well beyond the
capabilities of societies in any other historical era. Technology and industrial strategy are the keys, not the ideology.

But at what cost? Both models are equally confronted with two
major stresses, both of which threaten to topple industrial society: the
waste of industrial society and the depletion of the very resources upon
which they have built their success. SuperStock might well attenuate
ideological conflicts, but it solves neither of the above. We must solve
the problems of ideology, environment, resources and war. And we must
solve them concurrently.

We now are confronted with a resource base the real limits of which
are being probed. That resource base can no longer support the preten-
tions and appetites inherent to industrial society, as Lester Brown, Barry
Commoner and others have noted.[5] Both models rely upon future
growth to resolve social and economic problems. However, we are
moving into an age where increased resource exploitation can no longer
provide a growing pie, with correspondingly increased slices for all.

Thus, in addition to the surface conflict of ideology, we have a more
fundamental, severe and unavoidable conflict of the two world superpowers for access to the absolutely vital but rapidly diminishing
resource base. Unless we can, by the stroke of a magic wand, again obtain a new, unlimited resource base, we will confront violent crises. Or
we will be forced to create a non-industrial economic order. Or we will
perish.

Coveting material resources is a source of conflict between the two
superpowers every bit as fundamental as ideology. In this view ideology merely becomes a tool of the power mongers to enflame public
opinion in favor of accumulating and maintaining the huge military
machines necessary to protect access to the dwindling resources of this

planet. Thus, one can see the arms race as ultimately protecting the base of power for those who now enjoy it. To date our Trolls have been all too successful in their use of ideology to obfuscate the other issues. These power brokers cannot afford to let an idea like SuperStock defuse such a vital tool of power politics.

The Existential Crisis and Barriers to Overcoming It

The foregoing discussion can be summed up in six basic points:

(1) Social change has historically been through social violence or natural accident. Rarely has reason prevailed except as analysis after the fact.

(2) The power of the human intellect, as shown by its technological prowess, is being confronted with the paradox of limited natural abundance on the one hand. On the other is our transcendent technological capacity for annihilating violence embodied in nuclear weapons. This has brought humankind to a point of existential crisis: overcome violence or end the earth in an act of ultimate despair or accident.

(3) The power of this crisis is great—of unprecedented import. This potential will manifest itself either in a spasm of awesome violence or in an unprecedented transcendence of our basic nature. Crisis always catalyzes transcendent change, insist the authors of *Order Out of Chaos*.[6]

(4) We are also approaching a supply-vs-demand crisis over the planet's natural resources: its capital (non-renewable resources) and its sustaining systems (renewables—including food, fuels, water, climate and even atmosphere.) This crisis involves North/South as well as ideological and political divisions. Equitable resource distribution is not only a capitalist/Communist problem. It is also a rich/poor, powerful/weak problem.

(5) There are elements in the human community who enjoy tremendous power. These vested interests inevitably use their power to prevent change, if such change will seriously challenge their position of power. They also have substantial weaknesses, not the least of which is the blindness of greed.

(6) The human community is now beginning to grasp the potential of tools of the mind, tools of knowing and cooperation necessary to bring about the needed transcendence over violence. There are many efforts to develop systematically and apply these tools to our existential crisis.

Perhaps we can maintain the current stasis indefinitely. That is the hope of the power structure as represented by such apostles as Ronald Reagan. But there is far too much potential for survival and accomplishment within the human race for us to stand still. Such potential points to a possible age of abundance and fulfillment, only hinted at in utopian literature. It also holds within its terrible grasp the final end to the great human experiment.

Many are vitally concerned and offer excellent ideas and analyses, Speiser among them. Moreover, books like Marilyn Ferguson's *The Aquarian Conspiracy* or Fritzof Capra's *The Turning Point* announce the emergence of an astounding new reality, a new paradigm of change.[7] Our overly specialized, reductionistic bias in science, technology and politics, they argue, is on the verge of giving way to momentous, holistic and integrating theories: holistic, as ecology is to biology; obliterating absolute truth, as quantum physics does to classical physics; and redefining the primacy of consciousness, as it is beginning to be done at the boundaries of subatomic physics. Such discoveries at the frontiers of science point toward human potentials only perceptible to the dreamer.

But the cynic chides, "Dreamers, you're all just dreamers. Be realistic!" I say, "Why not dream? The alternative is catastrophe." And that catastrophe is all too close and probable to my taste. It is only the dreamers who can save us. Beware of the status quo's cynic who would freeze process that cannot be frozen. We are confronted today with transcendental choices. Let us dream of glory rather than continue to wallow in the stench of the cynic's "realistic" status quo.

MAD (Mutually Assured Destruction) is the codification and ultimate symbol of the current stasis. It allows the two mutually exclusive ideologies to coexist in precarious stalemate. This balance is, ironically, becoming ever more fragile through the marching advance of technology, a point tellingly made by Jonathan Schell in his celebrated *The Fate of the Earth*.[8] Speiser strives to sell SuperStock as a solution to this dilemma. His analysis of the nature of the ideological conflict is excellent. But he falls short in suggesting ideology as the essential barrier to resolving the conflict between the US and the Soviet Union.

The bases of that conflict are more complex. Here are 10 major barriers to resolving the nuclear nightmare. They are presented in the approximate order of their importance in preventing resolution of the Soviet-US conflict. A number of authors have examined these barriers, including Freeman Dyson, *Ground Zero*, George Kennan, Amory and L. Hunter Lovins and F. A. Wolf.[9]

(1) *The Power of the Military-Industrial Complex in Both Superpowers.* This is a problem of human nature and social organization, a mixture of greed and lust for power. It grows out of the historical experiences and economic accidents of both nations.

(2) *Geopolitical, Geoeconomic Competition.* Given that the earth is a finite planet, the real limits of which are becoming ever more apparent, the superpowers cannot avoid confrontation over competition for scarce natural resources and markets, nor over the international relationships necessary to securing those resources and markets.

(3) *International Balance of Power.* After the fall of Germany and Japan at the end of World War II, some nation had to assume the responsibility of restraining the growth of American global power.

(4) *Ideology.* Each nation is the dominant representative of one of the two major political economies of the world. Their ideologies seem to be mutually exclusive and irreconcilably hostile. Ideologies serve to legitimate hostilities. Leaders fan ideological conflict when they are under stress due to other failures, notably economic. (See number 7 below.)

(5) *National Insecurities.* Both nations have different national security concerns which arise from their own unique historical vulnerabilities. Soviet insecurities stem from this landbound nation's long history of brutal invasions. The United States' insecurities stem from its nearly losing the Second World War and its political belief that the cause was an inadequately prepared military.

(6) *The Obscene Size of the Existing Superpower Arsenals.* The magnitude of the mutual threats to each society, and to the planet in general, leads to extreme emotions of fear and distrust.

(7) *Government's Need for an Enemy.* This problem is as old as

government. When things go badly, as they often do (especially in times of crisis), human leadership always needs someone to blame.

(8) *Military Strategic Planning.* A fundamental maxim of modern military strategic theory is always to assume worst-case scenarios in planning for your opponent's military capability. This logic leads unavoidably to an automatically escalating arms race.

(9) *Strategic Models and Language.* The differences in historical experiences and language have led to the development of contrasting strategic models which, if not actually antithetical, greatly exacerbate misunderstanding of each other's intent.

(10) *Soviet Government Style.* The Soviet propensity for secrecy, international intrigue, lack of commitment to unverifiable aspects of international agreements and domestic police-state tactics may be understandable given their historical background. However, this behavior antagonizes Western leaders who condemn the open use of such tactics (conveniently overlooking their own covert use of some of these same tactics!). (Western leaders also make such Soviet behavior politically useful by transforming Soviet acts into rhetorical instruments for inflaming public passions.)

An effective plan for overcoming our existential crisis must deal with each major barrier lest that barrier become a tool for the plan's undoing in the hands of its opponents. Identifying barriers to the solution of our economic and ecological problems is also important but beyond the scope of this essay. Interestingly, but not surprisingly, such barriers are closely linked to the above. An adequate plan must involve synergistic solutions to our economic and ecological problems as well.

The first in my list of barriers, and one examined closely by Peter Navarro in his previously mentioned book, is the power of the military-industrial complex, the quintessential example of vested interests at work.[10] A dangerous blindness of those who propose solutions to the arms race is the urge to appropriate the huge income of the military-industrial complex in implementing their ideal world. Workable plans must appear to preserve the military-industrial complex's immediate access to its existing income stream. Intelligently synergistic plans will eventually make this huge drain of wealth less necessary.

Let us evolve a new and beneficial charter for the military industrial complex. Rather than continuing as guardians of the rickety old "defense" structure, let us assure them of continued profitability in championing the construction of the new. The Strategic Defense Initiative (SDI or Star Wars) is an appropriate and near-ideal intermediate occupation with which to distract the military-industrial complex while we move the superpowers toward meaningful arms reductions. In the process we would also be redirecting our gross military investments toward the desirable end of opening access to an unknown but possibly large resource base in space in the view of analysts, such as Ben Bova and General Daniel Graham.[11] In the eyes of advocates of peace, it may not be the best possible investment. But it is certainly far better than continued spending on more offensive nuclear weapons and further fraying of the nuclear trigger!

Consider the shift in military strategy that SDI implies. By acquiescing to an SDI development/nuclear arms reduction package, the military-industrial complex is in effect admitting the strategic and moral bankruptcy of a defense dependent upon nuclear offense. It is an implicit admission that the anti-nuclear community is right, that nuclear weapons are out of control. Such an admission is clearly an important tool to those who would remake the world in a less violent image.

The Synergy of Problems and Solutions

The foregoing is only one example of how problems and solutions intersect in complex ways. We urgently need a composite strategy which could, only as a whole, resolve problems intractable to solution by any one of the components. There is an essential power to be derived from an eclectic and comprehensive strategy that is not amenable to piecemeal approaches. Only a carefully interwoven strategy can offer the vital synergy necessary to command a sufficiently wide political appeal.

Both problems and solutions are synergistic in nature. This is predominately because of their relationship to hope—that quintessentially human quality—a quality unique to the only species known to look into its future, however dimly.

The synergism of the great problems of late 20th century life has led many to give up any hope of their resolution. It is a source of the great political apathy that impairs our society's vigor. It is a source of the alienation of American and Soviet youth, as manifested in their drug and their punk rock rebellions. It is a source of a record number of suicides and alcoholism in both the US and the USSR.

Fortunately, there is also a synergism in mutually reinforcing, multiple solutions. Perceived solvability is the essential first step. As the public begins to see how the solutions interrelate and are mutually reinforcing, the proposed strategy will gather momentum.

Many solutions to these great problems are being proposed, each with proponents who are so stuck to a specific worldview that they have denied themselves the essential mental facility necessary to create the vital eclectic solution—intellectual openmindedness. This is the trap of reductionism. We must carefully guard against the intellectual chauvinism characterized by nay-saying. It is far too easy to show why something cannot work; far harder, yet far better, to show how something might work if we made this or that adjustment and/or alliance.

Here are two mental tools which can be brought to bear on the process. The first is the process of imagining the future. We certainly cannot hope to lead ourselves consciously into a future we cannot imagine. Some suggest that it is the very process of imagining a future, the building in the mind of a specific future model and of the necessary bridges to get there, that is the essential ingredient in actually creating that future. Authors such as Maxwell Maltz argue that the human mind is a kind of servomechanism which will automatically carry out a well-thought-out plan if its paths and bridges are sufficiently detailed and realistic.[12]

The second tool is derived from a theory of successful negotiations. Roger Fisher and William Ury (among others) are developing a structured process for developing "win/win" solutions. The key ingredient for the successful negotiator, according to Roger Fisher and his associate William Ury, is achieving a thorough understanding of both sides of an issue, an understanding in which one tries, to the extent of his abilities, "to get into his opponent's shoes."[13] The problem is that most partisans subconsciously realize the risk to their own dearly held biases that a thorough understanding of the other side's position might entail. They therefore avoid it at all costs.

The key in this approach to negotiations for our process of inventing a workable and desirable future is to seek out and/or create win/win alliances. Detailed, open-minded knowledge of the other's position is essential to perceiving win/win opportunities. We must maintain this openmindedness in order to accept the essential less-than-ideologically-pure solution.

Consider this combined scenario which uses features from the Nuclear Weapons Freeze, the President's Strategic Defense Initiative (SDI) and an adaptation of the SuperStock strategy. SDI becomes a rational approach only if both nations participate and pace each other in development and deployment. The logic of the SDI fails if one side gets a substantial lead in effective defense over the other. This position would lead both to a terribly unstable need to strike first, with the leader believing he can withstand a weakened retaliation and the straggler thinking he must "use them or lose them." In the eyes of such critics as Zbigniew Brzezinski and John Tirman, this is what is so terrifying about the SDI as it is now proposed.[14]

A shared SDI becomes a form of mutually assured survival. It totally changes the equation in a way that should be acceptable to arms controllers.[15] In this scenario the anti-nuclear political forces would offer to support the initial development phases of the SDI in the interest of a renewed national defense consensus if the President would agree to the following concessions:

(1) That the President immediately attempt to negotiate a Nuclear Weapons Freeze (offensive *and* defensive) with the Soviets, with strong verification provisions.

One aspect of SDI that the arms-control community fears most is a dual offensive and defensive arms race. Only those of the arms control community who most covet the defense budget would be intransigent about any compromise. This strategy would unmask the most covetous. Such a SDI/Freeze should be acceptable (or at least, less objectionable) to the military-industrial complex as it would not threaten continued government contracts. We would also be calling the Soviet's bluff with respect to their professed willingness to freeze nuclear weapons.

(2) That coupled to this Nuclear Weapons Freeze agreement be the joint development with the Soviet Union of a space-based command and control system for a possible future space-based ballistic missile defense.

Since the President has already offered to share a completed technology with the Soviets, why not propose a joint development where the Soviets help develop the system and share in its development costs? Shared development should be of considerable interest to the Soviets who have historically felt technologically inferior. This strategy would give them first-hand knowledge of our technology (and vice versa!) This strategy would also unmask Reagan's offer to share in the event it is merely a political ploy. We would first develop and deploy the superior command, control, communications and intelligence systems that the SDI requires. Such systems would offer greatly enhanced space-based Freeze verification. Shared development would also build essential trust, as the scientific, engineering and political communities of the two nations learn to work successfully together in eliminating the nuclear nightmare.

(3) That the Freeze agreement include a clause that neither side will unilaterally deploy space-based armaments under the following conditions: (a) no cheating on the Freeze, (b) progress toward arms reduction and (c) joint agreement for partial deployment for protection from third parties (e.g., Qaddafi or Khomeini).

If the Freeze is successful and substantial arms reductions occur, we will save major deployment costs. Ideally, the deployment cost need cover only the minimum system necessary to cover small remaining arsenals, and as insurance to protect all from irrational madmen. The Soviets should also like this as it would give them voice in forestalling the part of SDI that they most fear—space-based weapons.

(4) SDI funding would be distributed on a priority basis to those companies who were willing to establish a SuperStock-like capital formation program. License rights to any American technological fallout would accrue to SuperStock.

As recommended by Speiser, our government could generate much publicity about the US commitment to SuperStock as "recognizing the need to democratize capital." This could be presented as an acknowledged *quid pro quo* for the substantial steps that the Soviet leader Gorbachev has made in privatizing the Soviet economy. There is likely to be much more technological and economic fallout from such extensive fundamental research into space defenses than the minimal economic fallout from further refinement of our offensive technologies, as such previously cited authors as Bova and Graham contend.[16] We can, for example, use new space transport systems to set up solar power satellites and/or space-based materials mining, processing and manufacturing. The Congress should grant full financial rights to this fallout to the new SuperStock program as a way to speed its promised benefits.

Such a synergistic plan would have widespread political appeal. It would undercut the impact of hostile constituencies and offer its proponents a political accomplishment of immense and lasting effect. The government would sell the strategy as a consensus vision with broad emotional appeal—a "shared mission for the good of all mankind." In this strategy the SDI would function as the "diversionary bone" for the military-industrial complex, buying their active cooperation and enlisting their formidable public relations tools. It would also make a substantial portion of our investment in "defense" aid in the commercial opening of the space frontier. Such a new resource base might make industrialism viable for centuries and could reduce competition for dwindling terrestrial resources.[17]

I do not propose the above as a final plan, only as a possible initial seed. Much study, analysis and dialogue must go into the development of such a synergistic, eclectic strategy. Only together can we weave an adequate tapestry, one that is up to the formidable task of achieving peace and justice in our time. Speiser's essential contribution may ultimately not be putting forth SuperStock itself, but stimulating the creation of a network for the initiation, integration and evaluation of synergistic ideas for grappling with the primordial problems of human survival in the late 20th century. Speiser himself hints at this possibility in the afterword of his book.

Editor's Comments

Marshall is convinced that we must solve the problems of ideology, environmental degradation, access to resources and war concurrently. The editor argued in his own essay that when we attempt to correct instances of economic injustice by itself, we ignore powerful forces that could neutralize the effectiveness of a scheme for greater justice, such as a plan for universal capitalism. In that essay emphasis was placed upon debt, pollution and population growth as the most likely neutralizing forces. Marshall has expanded this list in his "barriers to resolving the nuclear nightmare." To overcome these barriers he states that we need a synergistic solution.

The initial step in this quest is a process of imagining a preferred or desired future and how it can be achieved. The importance of this step cannot be overemphasized. Research in psychology has found that people tend to believe a hypothetical future event is more likely if they are presented with a sequence of events that would make it occur. It is tragic that our mass media spends so much time depicting every international crisis imaginable, including nuclear war, yet it pays minuscule attention to scenarios of peace. It is little wonder why most people consider lasting peace to be unattainable.

There are other approaches to dealing with the issues of economic injustice and the nuclear arms race which we have not discussed. John Perry's National Dividend Plan, the Sabre Foundation's "capital formation plan," and James Meade's "labor-capital partnership" and "social dividend" concepts are some examples of existing proposals to reform capitalism.[18] They all share the quality of not addressing larger, contextual problems, such as Larry Marshall's "barriers to resolving the nuclear nightmare" with which we have been concerned with in this book. This does not mean that these "fine-tuning" proposals do not have a place in the final "synergistic solution." All options deserve a fair hearing in our quest for addressing the "problematique humaine."

Gerald Mische's essay, "SuperStock and World Order: A Natural Partnership," probes yet another option.

Contribution by Gerald Mische

No sane thinker wants World War III to intervene to save the United States from the economic/monetary collapse which seems increasingly possible in the 1990s. What is our recourse? Not much—at least for the present. Until we develop effective international governance structures with the means and authority to cope with the new global realities of our interdependent world economy, our faith for preventing or surviving another economic collapse currently can be vested only in the structures and laws that, because they are national in scope, are not up to the task.

Our challenge then is to provide an alternate reading of the signs. We must help people recognize that many of the crises the human community is experiencing today are the growing pains of *growth*. They are pains of the struggle to negotiate a historic *structural transition* into a new future.

Global technologies and economic-monetary forces now encircle the planet. But parallel institutions capable of managing or "governing" the multiple ramifications of these new global realities are still in their embryonic stages. The result is a *structural gap* not only accounted for by the natural time it takes institutions to follow events but also related to a lag in worldview.

The historical challenge we face is not to "give up" sovereignty, but rather to *redefine* it. In so redefining sovereignty, we will find ourselves also redefining *security*.

In today's global village it is only possible to regain a viable sovereignty by pooling certain functional dimensions of sovereignty. As Emery Reves has put it: "The question is not one of 'surrendering' national sovereignty. The problem is not negative and does not involve giving up something we already have. The problem is positive—creating something we lack, but that we imperatively need."[19]

The task, then, is not to turn back to the past; nor is it to dismantle or bypass the nation-state, or to centralize power at a global level. Rather, the task is to recognize that, in today's interdependent world, both *private* and *public* sector institutions are needed at every level. The functional institutions that are required at the international should be structured according to the principle of *subsidiarity*.

With subsidiarity as the criterion for world order, decision making would be made at the lowest possible level. Only when problems cannot be managed and justice cannot be achieved at municipal, provincial or national levels are effective juridical institutions necessary at the regional or global level.

Such a world order is not a quantum jump into the unknown. It is, rather, the next logical step in social evolution.[20]

Mische is one of a few essayists who wrote about the need for some type of world federation, or strengthening of existing supranational organizations in relation to the issues of economic democracy and world peace. Another is Arnold Bergier who objects to Stuart Speiser's failure to investigate the economic rewards of world federation. He writes:

> If the nation states no longer had to rely on national armies for international security, most of the armed forces around the world could be disbanded, retaining only sufficient numbers to police their own states. National police would not need supersophisticated weaponry, and *all* the atomic weapons could be dismantled.[21]

In yet another approach to grappling with humankind's overwhelming problems, Thomas Moore offers an inspiring suggestion in his essay entitled, "Entering a New Age: How to Get There from Here." In discussing the world debt crisis Moore notes that the austerity measures forced upon a debtor nation by the International Monetary Fund (IMF) hurt the poor in those nations more than anyone else. He suggests that the SuperStock concept could be used to ease the plight of the poor in these countries.

Contribution by Thomas Moore

This could be done in several ways. Many private companies

in developing countries are forced to turn to foreign banks to finance capital projects because of the inadequacy of financial institutions in their own countries. The banks have been increasingly demanding that these loans be guaranteed by the government of the developing country. This results in the government having a great deal of influence over who receives the foreign loans (as well as the policies and projects implemented by the recipients of the loans) at the least, and complete nationalization of the enterprise where the government just assumes control of the company at most. The government could, at this point, add another step to the process—turning its shares of the company stock and other government-owned enterprises into shares of SuperStock in order to provide income for those outside of the economic elite and to use part of the dividends to repay the loans. This could be divided in the following manner: 45 per cent to individuals, 45 per cent to the banks to repay the loans used to finance SuperStock, and 10 per cent to be treated as a sort of excise tax to be used to pay the foreign debt and rescue the banking system from collapse.[22]

Ostensibly, the IMF could facilitate this process by promoting the USOP concept verbally, as well as backing it with currency or SDRs (Special Drawing Rights). Of course, the member nations of the IMF would have to agree with this approach since it would signify a major change in IMF policy. The World Bank was not mentioned by the essayists, but it would be an ideal international organization for promoting the USOP concept in the developing world.

How to adapt and strengthen international institutions so as to make them more effective instruments in the pursuit of economic justice and world peace is a perplexing question. Unfortunately, world federation is not a viable solution. The power of the United Nations might be slightly increased, but with today's definition of the nation state, and anxiety over the erosion of territorial sovereignty, little more can be expected.

There is a consensus of sorts among many essayists that the focus for change must presently be fixed on individuals and social institutions. As these change, the foundations for a more peaceful and world order today, and perhaps a world federation tomorrow, will naturally be laid. In other words, achieving world federation is seen as being an evolutionary process. There are no means to jump to it, yet there are many ways of moving slowly toward it.

Some of these are rooted in the American tradition. They are deeply imprinted on our institutions and our way of life, as Christopher Budd wrote in his essay:

> America does not represent a social nirvana anymore than Russia
> does. What America does represent is a direction for mankind that is
> truer to the individual. Though this path has become contorted and
> overgrown, and the journey along it made difficult, it remains the
> road to choose. The need is to cut away the entanglements that cover
> it and, perhaps, to check and if necessary to correct its alignment.[23]

Thomas Jefferson's name appears many times throughout the
Speiser Contest essays. Time and again Jefferson referred to America
as an experiment based upon the notion that *nothing* is unchangeable
but the inherent and inalienable rights of man. From the vantage point
of the late 18th century, Jefferson conceived of the ideal society being
an agrarian economy in which everyone owned sufficient land to be a
voter. In those days land was the principal means for accumulating
wealth and acquiring the right to vote. Jefferson's ideal society embodied widespread distribution of income-generating property and
therefore political representation. Democracy to him meant "the absence of hereditary or arbitrary class distinctions or privileges relating
to the common people." Jefferson's dream for America spanned both
the concepts of political *and* economic democracy. He and the other
founders of this nation built this conception of democracy into the
Declaration of Independence and the Constitution. It is still there, lying
dormant, awaiting its resurrection.

What went wrong is best described in the words of two of the essayists, Donald Clark and Kevin Ketchum.

Contribution by Donald Clark

America's foundation is freedom, that is, individual liberty with
a minimum of external control. This ideal was enshrined in the
Constitution at a time when American society was composed
of socioeconomic units of moderate size in which the exercise
of power by aggressive action was restrained by narrow boundaries and by the high degree of geographic, economic and social isolation which separated region from region. Everything
was local, including the responsibility for assuring social and
economic justice for all. It was therefore assumed that freedom
would be exercised within the social restraints imposed by lo-
calized society.

This worked well until the second half of the 19th century. At
that point, new technologies for travel and communications

began to generate an expansive environment in which supra-local organizations could flourish. In Europe this became the occasion for building politically centralized nations, but in America, with a constitutionally mandated low-profile political federation firmly in place, the exploitation of this new possibility became an economic challenge. Business rapidly built national or continental structures which were far more powerful and effective than the strictly limited regulatory authority of the federal system. Journalistic muckraking and bureaucratic trustbusting were early efforts to counter monopolistic abuses and to promote social justice.

The collapse of this centralized economic system in 1929, and the depression which followed, created a social crisis which forced the development of an equally centralized political authority. The New Deal was a necessity. An institutionalized concern for justice at the federal level had to be created to restrain the enormous power of business. Conservatives, who passionately opposed Roosevelt's program, have been scorned by both popular and academic comment as social neanderthals who fought against liberal measures designed to alleviate human suffering. Yes, *but,* they were also fighting for the American tradition of decentralized power and local control. They saw the growth of federal power as an attack on "freedom" and a threat to the genius of American society.

They were right, but they were also doomed to lose. History's tide was still generating a flow of power toward the evolving center, and in the United States this tide would continue in full force until the muscle of the political structure caught up with that of the economic. The intense pressures generated by the conduct of World War II accelerated the growth of government and by 1945 an alliance between equals had been forged by centralized business and centralized government, a partnership which produced the astonishing prosperity of the post-war decades. For a few short years it all worked; indeed, it seemed that the American economy had achieved the miracle of perpetual affluence.[24]

Contribution by Kevin Ketchum

The most fundamental right of a distinctively capitalist country like the US is the right to acquire and dispose of productive property, including the right to hire or dismiss the labor power of others. We like to say that "freedom," or "liberty," is our most precious right. This tends to take the form of a formal negative right to do what one wants, free from government constraints, irrespective of the wants and needs of others. There are constraints only insofar as they limit an individual's right to constrain the rights of others.

But this type of freedom is essentially a pre-condition, protected by procedural safeguards, which allows the acquisition and disposition of productive property to satisfy an individual's material needs and wants to an extent heretofore only enjoyed by monarchs who had kingdoms full of subjects to toil for them. The alleged benefit of capitalism is to allow any of us to live like kings if we can manage to accumulate productive property and employ wage labor to produce goods and make a profit through distribution in the "free market." Thus, the freedom we really cherish in the United States consists of the right to "enterprise" with our productive property "free" from government interference.

The problem with this capitalist system of ours, as it now exists, is that the capitalist's dream described above is not attainable by most citizens of the United States. Social consciousness lags behind social need in this regard. There is a social need to close the widening wealth gap in our nation, but the social consciousness that prevails is the belief that freedom from undue constraints provides equality of opportunity by which anyone can become affluent. The fallacy of this consciousness is that it disregards non-governmental constraints on a person's freedom to better his economic position. In a capitalist system wealth is power, and when such private power is wielded in a market essentially devoid of any social planning, those who are already affluent tend to increase their wealth at the expense of those who have been most instrumental in its accumulation—the wage laborers. What greater constraint on personal economic betterment can there be than to lose one's job because of employer relocation to provide a greater profit for the already affluent stockholders?[25]

Jefferson's dream of democracy has not come true for America. Still, America's story is only partially written. The legacy of such men as Thomas Jefferson lives in the hearts of all the essayists who wrote for this contest. Our hope is that the educational process has instilled in people an awareness of the principles upon which this nation was founded. Our goal is to nurture this awareness to critical mass so that a renaissance of the notion of Jeffersonian democracy, a renaissance of social imagination, will appear. Given this and political democracy, change will follow.

Norman Douglas once wrote: "A man who reforms himself has contributed his full share toward the reformation of his neighbor." American events continue to have a tremendous impact in the world. Economic reform which brings us closer to economic democracy will resound like thunder throughout the world. As long as the promotion of economic justice is pursued within the quest for broader, synergistic solutions to humankind's problems, with an accompanying and genuine "realignment" of societal values, enhanced prospects for world peace will surely follow.

EPILOGUE

by

Stuart M. Speiser

As I write this in the fall of 1987, Ronald Reagan stands before the United Nations as a great peacemaker, while the United States and the Soviet Union are seriously negotiating the first agreement in history to reduce nuclear weapons.

It is apparent that this movement toward political and military accommodation is at least partially propelled by economic factors. The Communist nations, led by the Soviet Union and China, and the capitalist nations, led by the United States, have been moving toward economic convergence for more than a decade, due to the imperfections that each sees in its own system. Gorbachev's opening to the West is motivated in part by his realization that the outmoded bureaucracy of communism is weakening the ability of the Soviet Union to compete as a serious industrial power. Furthermore, the costs of maintaining the nuclear arms race are borne by the Soviet people in reduced living standards.

This economic convergence, which in turn reduces ideological friction, has been a positive factor in opening the way for progress on arms reduction. As *Time* magazine noted in its cover story of July 27, 1987, Soviet adventurism and international proletarianism have been curtailed by the realization under Gorbachev that their economic system does not work well at home. *Time* observed that the Soviet state can no longer offer ideological inspiration to the world and, in the words of a Soviet diplomat, "there is less of a temptation to enforce our own model on others, because we are questioning our own model." *Time* went on to comment:

> If, perchance, some of the ideological underpinnings of that struggle are beginning to fade away, the rivalry could become far more manageable. Unlike other great international rivals, the U.S. and the Soviets have little serious conflict over commercial markets. And despite the struggle for political influence, both sides share an interest in calming certain regional disputes, like the Iran-Iraq war.[1]

In his speech of November 2, 1987, marking the 70th anniversary of the Bolshevik Revolution, Mikhail Gorbachev divorced the Soviet Union from the Trotsky specter of "hostile capitalist encirclement" and said that the inevitability of conflict between communism and capitalism was giving way to a new era of cooperation in a world that is now "interrelated, interdependent, and integral." And in his speech of December 8, 1987, on arrival at the White House for the treaty ceremony, Gorbachev observed:

> We in the Soviet Union have made our choices. We realize that we are divided not only by the ocean but also by profound historical, ideological, socioeconomic and cultural differences. But the wisdom of politics today lies in not using those differences as a pretext for confrontation, enmity, and the arms race.[2]

Gorbachev struck the same note in his ground-breaking book, *Perestroika:*

> It is impossible to move toward more harmonious relations between the U.S. and the USSR while being mesmerized by ideological myths.

> We certainly do not need an "enemy image" of America, neither for domestic nor for foreign policy interests. An imaginary or real enemy is needed only if one is bent on maintaining tension, on confrontation with far-reaching and, I might add, unpredictable consequences.[3]

In that remarkable book Gorbachev emphasized Lenin's flexible approach to achieving the goals of socialism, even if this meant discarding collective experiments in favor of policies that satisfied individual interests, such as Lenin's New Economic Policy which revived some aspects of capitalism in the Soviet Union of the 1920s.[4]

Since I wrote *How To End the Nuclear Nightmare* in 1984,[5] there have been other indications that ideology is one of the barriers to peaceful Soviet-American relations. British historian Hugh Thomas produced the first volume of a definitive work on the postwar East-West conflict, *Armed Truce,* in 1987. There Thomas asserts that the prime cause of the cold war was "the ideology of the Soviet leaders, and their consequent incapacity, rather than their reluctance to make permanent arrangements with the leaders of the capitalist states."[6]

The 1984-85 essay contest on universal capitalism posed the question of how we could modify American capitalism to lessen its ideological conflict with Soviet communism, and thereby open the way for nuclear disarmament. Unexpectedly, the movement has come from the Soviet side; but suppose that the United States reciprocated by removing some of the exploitation from capitalism. Given the dramatic 1987 progress, could we not expect to improve even more the chances for disarmament if we lessened the ideological tensions still further? In my opinion this would require development of a viable plan for universal capital ownership, which is the threshold problem of the essay question.

I was delighted at the response to the call for essays. The project got a big boost when I was fortunate enough to be a guest on Dennis Wholey's talk and call-in show, *Late Night America,* which is carried by public TV stations throughout the United States and Canada. There were many stimulating calls, and the Council on International and Public Affairs received hundreds of requests for essay entry forms. Some 300 papers were submitted, and all were read by panels of volunteers recruited from CIPA's board of trustees by President Ward Morehouse.

The high intellectual content of the essays exceeded my wildest hopes. On top of that, Professor Kenneth Taylor's undertaking to produce this book was a bonanza for progress toward universal capitalism. My incomplete vision of a plan for universal share ownership, and the even more obscure connection between American capital ownership and the possibilities for world peace, were greatly enhanced by the essayists and by Ken Taylor's synthesis.

Another immediate benefit from this project has been the privilege of meeting Professor Jon Wisman, the winning essayist, and Professor Ken Taylor. Both of these scholars have stated that they are going to spend a good part of their future careers on subjects related to the theme of this contest. That in itself is a great reward and I am sure that it will lead to important progress.

Encouraged by the results of this contest, we decided to continue the project. In 1986 there were two more contests, this time focused on the mechanics of plans for universal share ownership, without considering its relevance to the nuclear nightmare. The 1986 project included an American competition under the sponsorship of the Council on International and Public Affairs, as well as a British counterpart sponsored by the Wider Share Ownership Council. The prize-winning essays have been selected and the best of the American and British entries will be published by the Council on International and Public Affairs in late 1988.

Building on this progress, a 1988 contest will again cover the United States and Great Britain, under sponsorship of CIPA and WSOC respectively, with separate prizes. The 1988 topic will be, "How can we use broadened share ownership to alleviate the problems of unemployment, under-employment and poverty-level wages?" Those entering the 1988 contests will have the benefit of this volume as well as the volume devoted to the 1986 essays.

As Professor Taylor has noted, the combination of two complicated ideas—universal capital ownership and the ideological underpinnings of Soviet-American hostility—makes for a lot of controversy. It certainly made the essay competition more complicated, but I do not regret this decision. It opened the minds of many peace seekers to another potential tool, and there are not so many tools around capable of bringing world peace that we can afford to ignore even those whose relevance may appear questionable on the surface.

Professor Taylor concluded: "As long as the promotion of economic justice is pursued within the quest for broader, synergistic solutions to humankind's problems . . . enhanced prospects for world peace will surely follow."[7] His statement echoes the words of the Reverend Martin Luther King, Jr.: "True peace is not merely the absence of tension; it is the presence of justice."

APPENDIX

Cost Analysis of the Modified SuperStock Plan

by

John Sedlak

The following population data are from the *National Data Book and Guide to Sources: Statistical Abstract of the U.S.*, 105th edition:[1]

Year 1983	In Millions
Total US Population	234.0
Under 18 Years of Age	62.5
18-64 Years of Age	144.1
Over 64 Years of Age	27.4

The number of work-disabled persons age 18-64 is taken to be 13.1 million from the *National Data Book* (table 635)[2] for persons age 16-64 in 1982. The number of persons over 64 years of age, previously judged to be work-disabled at age 18-64, is calculated to be 6.6 million by taking 24.1 per cent (i.e., the per cent of persons age 55-64 who are work-disabled from table 635)[3] of the total population over 64 years of age (i.e., 27.4 million). The number of persons eligible for a modified SuperStock work-disability portfolio is thus taken to be 13.1 million plus 6.6 million, or 19.7 million.

The number of unemployed persons seeking government-created jobs (GCJs) under modified SuperStock is assumed to be 12 million. The current number of unemployed persons seeking work is about 8 million.[4] For the purposes of this analysis this figure is augmented to reflect: (1) a growing population, (2) increasing unemployment due to increasing automation and (3) additional persons who are seeking employment but who do not show up in the U.S. Department of Labor statistics. The offsetting effect of (1) the "baby boom" generation moving out of the labor market and (2) persons who are voluntarily unemployed or between jobs has also been figured into the 12 million person estimate.

The number of persons age 18-64 who are not work-disabled and are eligible to receive an annually augmented modified SuperStock portfolio is 131 million—i.e., the total population age 18-64 (144.1 million), less the number of work-disabled in the same age group (13.1 million).

The number of persons over 64 years of age who are eligible for a stock portfolio valued at $50,000 is calculated to be 20.8 million. This figure is obtained by subtracting the number of persons over 64 years of age who have previously been judged to be work-disabled (i.e., 6.6 million) from the total population over 64 years of age (27.4 million). Speiser's proposition[5] that a 5:1 stock value to annual stock dividend ratio is realizable if corporate income taxes are eliminated, and virtually all corporate earnings are paid out as dividends, is accepted as the basis for all financial calculations for modified SuperStock.

The annual cost of producing full employment opportunity via government-created jobs is calculated to be $450 billion. This figure is obtained by multiplying 12 million unemployed persons by $37,500 which is 2.5 times the average wage/benefit package of $15,000. A $2.25 trillion stock fund would be needed to produce the annual $450 billion cost, assuming a stock value to annual stock dividend ratio of 5:1.

To provide 19.7 million work-disabled persons with $60,000 stock portfolios, each generating about $12,000 annually, would require $1.182 trillion of appropriated stock. The number of work-disabled persons is assumed to be constant, with the annual number of deaths in this category assumed to be equal to the number of persons annually becoming eligible for work-disability portfolios. Since the appropriated stock would serve as a revolving fund, no increments are presumed necessary. A stock value to annual stock dividend ratio of 5:1 is assumed.

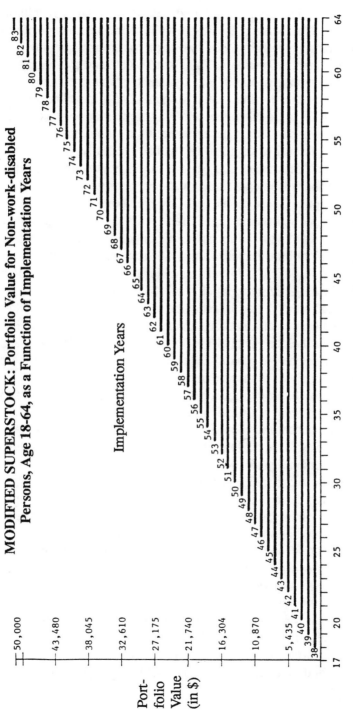

Figure A1

MODIFIED SUPERSTOCK: Portfolio Value for Non-work-disabled
Persons, Age 18-64, as a Function of Implementation Years

The total revolving stock fund needed to provide 131 million non-work-disabled persons age 18-64 with individual stock portfolios, incrementing annually by $1,087 worth of stock to a maximum of $50,000 at age 64, is $3.275 trillion. This figure is obtained by multiplying 131 million persons by $50,000 and dividing the product by two. Figure A1 shows the stock portfolio value for non-work-disabled persons at each age from 18 to 64 when the revolving stock fund for this category is fully developed. During development of this fund, the portfolio value at each age level (except age 18) will be gradually moving toward its maximum. This means that persons in this group during the development period will emerge from it with portfolios which have not reached the maximum. These people will, however, be moving into the next age category and so become eligible for a full $50,000 stock portfolio. The start-up cost of $143 billion is the amount of stock needed to give each of the 131 million persons in this category an initial stock increment valued at $1,087. The 45-year total increment of $3.132 trillion represents the total revolving stock fund ($3.275 trillion), less the start-up cost ($143 billion). The 5:1 ratio of stock value to annual stock dividend assumed here means that each annual stock increment should increase a portfolio holder's annual dividend income by about $218 and that when it reaches is maxim level, a portfolio would produce about $10,000 in dividend income in a year.

The cost of providing each of the 20.8 million persons over 64 years of age who were not previously work-disabled with a $50,000 stock portfolio, generating about $10,000 in annual dividend income, is calculated to be $1.04 trillion. This figure is obtained by multiplying 20.8 million persons by $50,000.

Figure A2 graphically summarizes modified SuperStock's financial picture. Line AB represents the cumulative amount of capital invested by American business in new plants and equipment. The annual rate of $300 billion dollars is accepted from Speiser.[6]

Lines CEF show the cumulative amount of stock appropriated for the modified SuperStock program at a rate of $150 billion per year. Notice that this appropriation assumes a seven year lag during which time the to-be-appropriated stock is held by a lender while the cost of its purchase is paid off. This seven-year amortization period is the minimum estimated by Speiser.[7] At point E, 59 years into modified SuperStock, no more appropriation of stock will be required except to replace defunct or diminished stock or to expand the program.

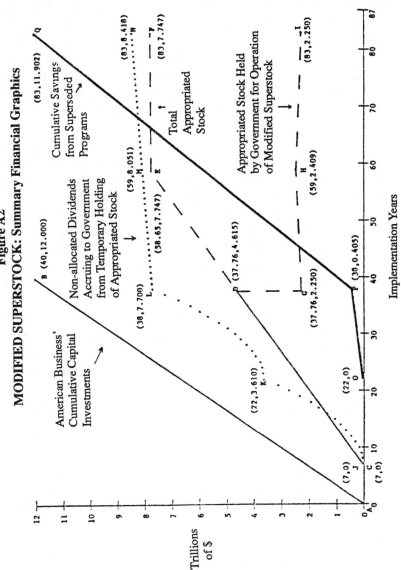

Figure A2
MODIFIED SUPERSTOCK: Summary Financial Graphics

Line CD represents the amount of appropriated stock temporarily held by the government until the start-up stock fund is acquired. Between D and G, this stock has been transferred to its beneficiaries, and the amount at G ($2.25 trillion) is that permanently held for the operation of the jobs portion of the program. Between G and H, an accumulation of temporarily held stock occurs since the annual appropriation of $150 billion exceeds the amount immediately needed (by $7.6 billion per year) for the annual increment to the portfolios of non-work-disabled persons age 18-64. At point H, the total stock fund has been acquired and the excess stock, temporarily held, is then distributed annually, as needed for the program, until at point I, $2.25 trillion of stock remains to be permanently held by the government for the operation of the government-created jobs portion of the program.

J through K, L, M and N represents the cumulative dividend income accruing to the government from the temporary holding of appropriated stock. At point K, 22 years into modified SuperStock, the government-created jobs portion of the program begins. The $2.25 trillion of appropriated stock accumulated to this point is then permanently applied to this operation. The geometric accumulation of dividends is then approximately repeated to point L, as the appropriated stock is temporarily held awaiting its build-up into a start-up fund for the other portions of the program. The accumulation of dividend income from L to N corresponds to the temporary holding of appropriated stock shown from G to I.

Line OP represents the cumulative savings realized from programs superseded by the establishment of full employment opportunity via GCJs. The annual savings of $25.3 billion realized during this period comes from the elimination of unemployment compensation and existing jobs and job training programs. This figure is calculated from the following data given in the *National Data Book and Guide to Sources.*[8]

	In Billions
Table 593:	
Total Expenditures for Jobs and Training (1983)	$ 4.169
Less Summer Youth Employment (1983)	0.721
Equals	3.448
Table 596:	
Amount of Unemployment Benefits (1982)	21.852

Line PQ shows the accumulated savings from all programs superseded by the operation of the total modified SuperStock program. The annual savings realized between P and Q is calculated to be $255.489 billion. The itemization below is again taken from the *National Data Book and Guide to Sources.*[9]

	In Billions
Table 593:	
Total Supplemental Security Income (1983)	$ 10.101
Pensions for Needy Veterans (1983)	3.894
Aid to Families with Dependent Children (1983)	15.385
Less 75 per cent	11.539
Equals	3.846
Table 596:	
Disability Benefits Total (1982)	44.750
Less Workers' Compensation	8.909
Less Temporary Disability	1.624
Equals	34.217
Survivor Monthly Benefits (1982)	42.800
Subtotal	230.189
Plus Savings from the Jobs Program	25.300
Equals	255.489

Figure A3 shows projections for the federal debt under five scenarios, with and without modified SuperStock. The 1985 federal debt is nearly $2 trillion. *Time* magazine stated in July 1985 that "it threatens to grow at the staggering annual rate of $200 billion for the rest of the decade."[10] Efforts, of course, are always being made to reduce the rate of growth of the debt. The projections shown in Figure A3, line A, assume that by 1992 the federal debt will be $3 trillion, and that without modified SuperStock, it will annually increase by the amount of its interest payment which is assumed to be 6.5 per cent of the current principal. With modified SuperStock in effect (line B) all dividends accruing to the government from its temporary holding of appropriated stock, and all savings that are realized from programs superseding modified SuperStock, are assumed to be applied *immediately* to the federal debt interest payment and principal, which is eliminated in 52 years.

Line C represents a budget-balanced, $3 trillion federal debt. Line D shows the effect of applying modified SuperStock's non-allocated dividends and superseded programs savings to the annual interest payment and principal, with any 6.5 per cent interest payment shortfall being covered by federal budget funds. Under this scenario, the federal debt is eliminated in 34 years. Line E shows the effect of applying these non-allocated dividends to paying off the federal debt principal, while all 6.5 per cent annual interest payments are covered by the federal budget. Under these conditions, the federal debt is abolished in 21 years.

All of the above financial estimates and projections for modified SuperStock are assumed to obtain, even as inflation reduces the real value of the dollar, because stock values and dividends would be expected to increase in proportion to inflation.

Figure A3
FEDERAL DEBT PROJECTIONS

(Assume 1986 as first year, during first 7 years, assume a
$143 billion average annual debt increment, including interest payment.)

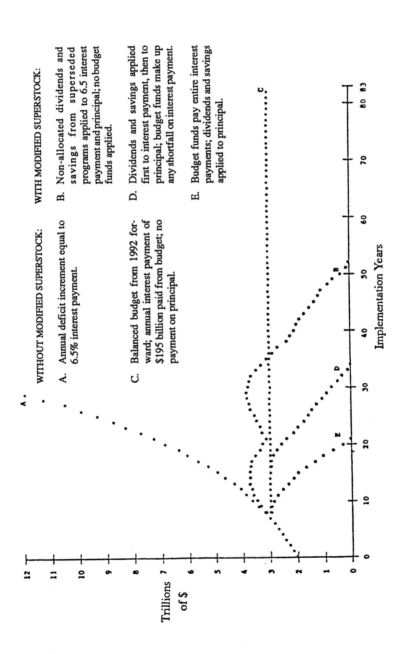

NOTES

(Citations for essays submitted in the 1984-85 Speiser Essay Contest on which this volume is based have been assumed to be unpublished, although their authors are free to do so, and have been identified here only by the author's name, title of essay and the designation "Speiser Contest Essay.")

1. The Stuart M. Speiser Essay Contest

1. Stuart M. Speiser, *The USOP Handbook: A Guide to Designing Universal Share Ownership Plans for the United States and Great Britain* (New York: Council on International and Public Affairs, 1986).
2. Earl Foell and Richard Nenneman, eds., *How Peace Came to the World* (Cambridge, MA: MIT Press, 1986).
3. Ibid., p. 56.
4. Lester C. Thurow, "Building a World-Class Economy," *Society*, 22, No. 1, p. 16.
5. Martin Weitzman, *The Share Economy: Conquering Stagflation* (Cambridge, MA: Harvard University Press, 1984).
6. Robert B. Reich, *The Next American Frontier* (New York: Times Books, 1983).
7. Larry Marshall, "Synergistic Solutions: A Tapestry of Great Power," Speiser Contest Essay, p. 9.
8. Stuart M. Speiser, *How to End the Nuclear Nightmare* (Croton-on-Hudson, NY: North River Press, 1984), pp. 9-10.
9. Jane Dillion, "Selling SuperStock," Speiser Contest Essay, pp. 15-16.

10. Donald Clark, "Devolution: A Path to Stable Peace," Speiser Contest Essay, pp. 8-9.
11. Speiser, *How to End Nuclear*, op. cit., p. 117.
12. For an interesting analysis of the impact of the computer in the workplace, see Lester Thurow, "Economic Paradigms and Slow American Productivity Growth," unpublished paper, MIT, Cambridge, MA, 1987.
13. Herman Kahn, William Brown and Leon Martel, *The Next 200 Years* (New York: William Morrow, 1976).
14. Foell and Nenneman, op. cit., p. 165.

II. Economic Reform for Humanity's Greatest Struggle

1. Jon D. Wisman, "Economic Reform for Humanity's Greatest Struggle," Speiser Contest Essay.
2. Stuart M. Speiser, *How to End the Nuclear Nightmare* (Croton-on-Hudson, NY: North River Press, 1984).
3. Ibid., p. 97.
4. Ibid., pp. 132, 165.
5. Ibid., p. 134.
6. Ibid., p. 9.
7. Ibid., p. 77.
8. Ibid., p. 102; also p. 10.
9. Peter Berger, *The Sacred Canopy* (New York: Doubleday, 1967), p. 22.
10. Speiser, op. cit., p. 97.
11. Ibid., p. 174.
12. Ibid.
13. The book that launched much of the most recent speculation on this question is Nobel Laureate Konrad Lorenz' *On Aggression* (London: Methuen, 1966).
14. See Charles J. Lumsden and Edward O. Wilson, *Promethean Fire* (Cambridge, MA: Harvard University Press, 1983), p. 160.
15. Richard E. Leakey and Roger Lewin, *People of the Lake* (New York: Avon Books, 1979), pp. 217, 236.
16. David P. Barash, *Sociobiology and Behavior*, 2nd ed. (New York: Elsevier, 1982), p. 352.
17. Cited in John G. Gurley, *Challengers to Capitalism*, 2nd ed. (New York: W.W. Norton, 1979), p. 110.
18. Although Speiser recognized that US and Soviet leaders might "resort to military action to compensate for poor economic perfor-

mance" *(How to End Nuclear,* op. cit., p. 104), he does not suggest how this might relate to his claim that ideology is the "root" cause of US-Soviet hostilities.

19. For an interesting discussion of the effect of climatic cycles on socioeconomic conditions, see E.L. Jones, *The European Miracle* (London: Cambridge University Press, 1981), especially Chapters 1 and 2.

20. Mancur Olson, *The Rise and Decline of Nations* (New Haven: Yale University Press, 1982).

21. Walter Laqueur, "The Day the World Stopped Believing Moscow," *Washington Post,* (September 28, 1986), p. C3.

22. Stanley Lebergott, *Manpower in Economic Growth: The American Record Since 1800* (New York: McGraw-Hill, 1964), p. 139.

23. John Stuart Mill, *Principles of Political Economy* [1848]. (Clifton, NJ: Augustus M. Kelly, 1973), pp. 760-61.

24. See, for instance, W.D. Nordhaus, "The Political Business Cycle," *Review of Economic Studies,* 42 (April 1975), pp. 169-90; Martin Paldam, "An Essay on the Rationality of Economic Policy: The Test Case of the Electional Cycle," *Public Choice,* 37 (November 1981), pp. 287-305; and Raford Boddy and James Crotty, "Class Conflict, Keynesian Policies, and the Business Cycle," *Monthly Review,* 26, No. 5 (October 1974), pp. 1-17.

25. Lorraine B. Blank, "The Impact of Workplace Participation: A Multivariate Analysis" (Ph.D. Dissertation), The American University, Washington, DC, 1985).

26. An estimate of the value of fixed non-residential private capital is found in US Bureau of the Census, *Statistical Abstract of the US, 1984* (Washington, DC: US Department of Commerce, 1984), p. 541.

27. Speiser, op. cit., p. 210.

28. Robert B. Reich, *The Next American Frontier* (New York: Times Books, 1983), p. 204.

29. Speiser, op. cit., pp. 194-207.

30. R. H. Tawney, *The Acquisitive Society* (New York: Harcourt, Brace & World, 1920); and Thorstein Veblen, *Absentee Ownership and Business Enterprise in Recent Times: The Case of America* (New York: B. W. Huebsch, 1923).

31. Speiser, op. cit., p. 211.

32. Ibid., p. 217.

33. Jerome Rabow and Lynn Sappington, "Modified Speiser Plan," Speiser Contest Essay, pp. 3-5.

34. Francis Kingen, "World Peace Through Monetary Systems Change," Speiser Contest Essay, pp. 3-5, 22.

III. Social Change and the Limits of Ideology

1. Karl Marx, *Capital*, Vol. I (Chicago: Charles H. Kerr, 1906), p. 197.
2. Karl Marx, *Capital*, Vol. 3 (New York: Vintage Books, 1981), p. 571.
3. Oskar Lange, "On the Economic Theory of Socialism" in B. E. Lippencott, ed., *On the Economic Theory of Socialism* (Minneapolis: University of Minnesota Press, 1938); also in Lange and Taylor, published by McGraw-Hill, New York, 1956..
4. James Mason, "Survival Is Our Business," Speiser Contest Essay.
5. Richard Nixon, *The Real War* (New York: Warner Books, 1980).
6. Freeman Dyson, *Weapons and Hope (New York: Harper & Row, 1984), pp. 190-91.*
7. Stuart M. Speiser, *How to End the Nuclear Nightmare* (Croton-on-Hudson, NY: North River Press, 1984), p. 9.
8. Dyson, op. cit.
9. Foy D. Kohler, *Understanding the Russians, A Citizen's Primer* (New York, Evanston & London: Harper & Row, 1970), p. 82.
10. Robert G. Kaiser, *Russia, the People and the Power* (New York: Athenum, 1976), p. 481.
11. Speiser, op. cit., pp. 265-66.
12. Kenneth K. Krough, "Making Universal Capitalism a Reality," Speiser Contest Essay.
13. Louis O. Kelso and Mortimer J. Adler, *The Capitalist Manifesto* (Westport, CT: Greenwood Press, 1958).
14. Corey Rosen, Katherine J. Klein and Karen M. Young, *Employee Ownership in America: The Equity Solution* (Lexington, MA: Lexington Books, D.C. Heath, 1986), p. 15.
15. Speiser, op. cit., pp. 201-02.
16. Ibid., p. 7.
17. Ibid., p. 207.
18. Ibid., p. 188.
19. Ibid., p. 63.
20. Ibid., p. 10.
21. Stuart M. Speiser, *SuperStock* (New York: Everest House Publishers, 1982), p. 212.
22. Christopher Budd, "The Metamorphosis of Capitalism," Speiser

Contest Essay, pp. 5-6.

23. Florian Zalewski, "Property and Peace: Exploring the Foundations of Widespread Capital Ownership," Speiser Contest Essay, pp. 10-15.

IV. Power, Ideology and Culture

1. On the differences among Marxism, Democratic Socialism, Leninism, Stalinism (and Khrushchev's interpretation) and the failure of the American leaders to distinguish much difference, see Michael Parenti, *The Anti-Communist Impulse* (New York: Random House, 1969). Unfortunately, this book tends to be ignored by American diplomatic historians, probably since Parenti sympathizes with radicalism. Interestingly, conservative John Lukacs (Hungarian-American) also denounces anti-communism as failing to understand that the principal danger is Russian arms, not Marxist ideology, in *Outgrowing Democracy: A History of the United States in the Twentieth Century* (New York: Doubleday, 1984).

2. Thomas G. Paterson, ed., *Major Problems in American Foreign Policy Since 1914*, Vol. II (Lexington, MA: D. C. Heath, 1984), p. 258.

3. Americans could profit from re-reading Jose Ortega y Gasset's *Revolt of the Masses* (New York: W. W. Norton, 1932). Its title is quite misleading. It is really critical of unlimited use of technology, and not a counter-revolutionary tract.

4. Robert Whealey, "How to Get Along with the Soviet Union," Speiser Contest Essay.

5. Paul Grenier, "The Common Task: Peace Through Convergence Toward Compatible Ideals," Speiser Contest Essay.

6. See especially, Semyon L. Frank, *Ocherk Metodologii Obshchestvennykh Nauk* (Moscow: Bereg, 1922).

7. See Pitirim Sorokin, "Fluctuation of Social Relationships, War, and Revolution" in *Social and Cultural Dynamics*, Vol. 3 (New York: Bedminster Press, 1962), Chapter 15. Data convincingly support the thesis that cultures which are predominately "sensate" or "ideational" have certainly existed. (See also definitions below.)

8. F.S.C. Northrup, *The Meeting of East and West* (New York: Macmillan, 1946).

9. Edwin M. Schur, *Law and Society: A Sociological View* (New York: Random House, 1968), p. 115.

10. This quotation and the two following are from Pitirim Sorokin,

Society, Culture and Personality: Their Structure and Dynamics (New York: Harper & Brothers, 1947), pp. 507-08.

11. Ibid., pp. 507-22; and Sorokin, *Dynamics,* op. cit., pp. 259-509, especially Chapters 11 and 14.

12. From Lenin's essay, "Left-Wing Communism—An Infantile Disorder" (emphasis mine), cited in Leszek Kolakowski, *Main Currents of Marxism,* Vol. 2 (Oxford: Oxford University Press, 1982), p. 504. Note likewise the innumerable placards in the USSR stating, "The People and the Party Are One!" This exaggerated unity at the expense of diversity is perhaps not so much a formal doctrine as an underlying perverse aesthetic.

13. From "Return Address Moscow," International News Bulletin on *Independent Peace Activity in the USSR,* 1, No. 2, p. 9.

14. Stuart M. Speiser, *How to Achieve Peace and Justice in Our Time: New Ideas for Ending the Nuclear Nightmare and Revitalizing the U.S. Economy* (New York: Council on International and Public Affairs, 1984), p. 27.

15. Michael Voslensky, *Nomenklatura: Gospodstvuyushchii klass Sovetskogo Soyuza [The Nomenklatura: The Soviet Ruling Class]* (London: Overseas Publications, 1984), p. 450.

16. Ibid., p. 435.

17. Speiser, *How to End Nuclear,* op. cit., p. 163.

18. Vladimir Solovyov, *The Justification of the Good* (New York: Macmillan, 1918), p. xii.

19. Ibid., p. 335.

20. Paramahansa Yogananda, *Autobiography of a Yogi* (Los Angeles: Self-Realization Fellowship, 1975), p. 265. The Hindu philosophy expressed in the *Autobiography* is a marvelous example of a universal and balanced idealistic philosophy in the sense used below.

21. *New York Times,* July 20, 1984.

22. In law the work of Leon Petrazycki, which for a variety of tragic reasons has gone nearly unnoticed, should prove important. Idealistic economic science will most likely start with the work of Aristotle, Solovyov, Steiner, Schumacher and, I hope, Jane Jacobs. See especially *Law and Morality: Leon Petrazycki* (Cambridge, MA: Harvard University Press, 1955).

23. For a definition of "familistic," see Sorokin, *Society, Culture,* op. cit., pp. 99-102.

24. Jane Jacobs, *Cities and the Wealth of Nations: Principles of Economic Life* (New York: Random House, 1985).

25. Jane Dillion, "Selling SuperStock," Speiser Contest Essay, pp. 5-6.

V. Land, Rent and Capital

1. Karl Marx, *Capital,* Vol. 3 (Chicago: Charles H. Kerr, 1906), pp. 731-32.
2. As quoted in Tertius Chandler, *Chandler's Half-Encyclopedia* (San Francisco: Gutenberg Press, 1983), p. 1625.
3. Steven Cord, "How Much Revenue Would a Full Land Value Tax Yield? Analysis of Census and Federal Reserve Data," *The American Journal of Economics and Sociology* (July 1985), p. 279.
4. Stuart M. Speiser, *How to End the Nuclear Nightmare* (Croton-on-Hudson, NY: North River Press, 1984), p. 10.
5. Fred Foldvary, "Peace with Economic Justice," Speiser Contest Essay, 1986.
6. Adam Smith, *The Wealth of Nations* [1776]. (New York: McGraw-Hill, 1973).
7. Henry George, *Progress and Poverty* [1879]. (Caanan, NH: Phoenix Publishers, 1979).
8. Jeffrey Smith, "Beyond Ideology and the Threat of Nuclear War—Geonomics," Speiser Contest Essay.

VI. Fine-Tuning the Concept of Universal Capitalism

1. Arthur Okun, as quoted in P. Samuelson and W. Nordhaus, *Economics,* 12th ed. (New York: McGraw-Hill, 1985), p. 744.
2. Lester C. Thurow, "The 'Big Trade-Off' Debunked: The Efficiency of a Fair Economy," *Washington Monthly* (November 1985), p. 54.
3. Kenneth B. Taylor, "The Alpha Proposal," Speiser Contest Essay.
4. Mihajlo Mesavoric and Edward Pestel, *Mankind at the Turning Point* (New York: Signet, 1976), p. 11
5. Ruth Leger Sivard, *World Military and Social Expenditures, 1983-85* (Leesburg, VA: WMSE Publications, 1985),
6. Mesarovic and Pestel, op. cit., p. 11.
7. D. L. Meadows, D. H. Meadows, J. Randers and W. Behrens III, *The Limits to Growth* (New York: Signet, 1972).
8. Thomas Jones, *Options for the Future: A Comparative Analysis of*

Policy-Oriented Forecasts (New York: Praeger, 1980).
9. Ibid., p. 234.
10. Mesarovic and Pestel, op. cit., p. 127.
11. Paul A. Samuelson, *Economics,* 11th ed. (New York: McGraw-Hill, 1980), p. 747.
12. Lester C. Thurow, "The Implications of Zero Economic Growth," *Challenge* (March/April 1977).
13. Ibid.
14. Creel Froman, *The Two American Political Systems: Society, Economics and Politics* (Englewood Cliffs, NJ: Prentice-Hall, 1984), p. 52.
15. Ibid., p. 54.
16. Geoffrey Barraclough, *An Introduction to Contemporary History* (New York: Pelican Books, 1967), p. 199.
17. Lester C. Thurow, *The Zero-Sum Society* (New York: Basic Books, 1980), p. 75.
18. Stuart M. Speiser, *How to End the Nuclear Nightmare* (Croton-on-Hudson: North River Press, 1984), pp. 61-96.
19. Ibid., pp. 187-88.
20. Ibid., pp. 188-89.
21. *U.S. News and World Report* (September 16, 1985), p. 34.
22. Ibid., p. 33.
23. Speiser, op. cit., pp. 129-47.
24. Ibid., p. 137.
25. Ibid., p. 144.
26. Ibid.
27. Ibid., p. 142.
28. Thurow, *Zero-Sum Society,* op. cit., p. 109.
29. Speiser, op. cit., p. 141.
30. R. Easterlin, *Population, Labor Force and Long Swings in Economic Growth: The American Experience* (New York: Columbia University Press, 1968).
31. Samuelson, *Economics,* 11th ed., op. cit., p. 539.
32. See Robert L. Heilbroner, *An Inquiry Into the Human Prospect* (New York: W. W. Norton, 1980), p. 175.
33. Herman Kahn et al., *The Next 200 Years* (New York: William Morrow, 1976).
34. See Heilbroner, op. cit.
35. Daniel Bell, *The Coming of Post-Industrial Society* (New York: Basic Books, 1973).
36. Barbara Blumberg, *The New Deal and the Unemployed: The View*

from New York City (Lewisburg, PA: Bucknell University Press, 1977), pp. 282-83.

37. Pope John Paul II, *Laborem Excerens (On Human Work)*. (Boston: Daughters of St. Paul, 1981), paragraphs 25 and 18 respectively.

38. National Conference of Catholic Bishops, "Catholic Social Teaching and the U.S. Economy" (2nd Draft) in *Origins*, 15, No. 17 (October 10, 1985), paragraph 136.

39. Congressional Budget Office, "Economic and Budget Outlook: FY 1986-FY 1990" (Washington, DC, February 1985), as cited in "Catholic Social Teaching and the U.S. Economy," op. cit., paragraph 141.

40. This figure comes from dividing the $82 monthly cost per man for WPA employment (from Arthur M. Schlesinger, Jr., *The Age of Roosevelt: The Politics of Upheaval* [Boston: Houghton Mifflin, 1960], p. 349) by the average nationwide WPA monthly pay of $55 per month (from Robert S. McElvaine, *The Great Depression: America 1929-41* [New York: Times Books, 1984], p. 266).

41. Basil Rauch, *The History of the New Deal* (New York: Octagon Books, 1980), p. 164.

42. Ibid.

43. Russell A. Nixon, "The Historical Development of the Conception and Implementation of Full Employment as Economic Policy" in David C. Colander, ed., *Solutions to Unemployment* (San Diego: Harcourt, Brace, Jovanovich, 1981), pp. 131-32.

44. Neysa Chouteau, "Toward Realizing the Dream: A Response to *How to End the Nuclear Nightmare*," Speiser Contest Essay.

45. Ibid., pp. 12-13.

46. James Albus, *People's Capitalism: The Economics of the Robot Revolution* (Kensington, MD: New World Books, 1976).

47. James Albus, "An Industrial Policy That Would Work . . . for Everyone," Speiser Contest Essay.

48. Donald Clark, "Devolution: A Path to Stable Peace," Speiser Contest Essay.

49. Kevin Ketchum, "Expanding the Democratic Ideal: A Redefinition of Free Enterprise," Speiser Contest Essay, pp. 7-8.

50. Ibid., p. 12.

51. Ibid., pp. 14-16.

52. Florian Zalewski, "Property and Peace: Exploring the Foundations of Capital Ownership," Speiser Contest Essay, p. 19. The cited proposal by Rothbard can be found in Murray Rothbard, *The*

Mystery of Banking (New York: Richardson & Snyder, 1983), pp. 263-69.

53. Francisco Muller, "From the Nuclear Nightmare to the American Dream," Speiser Contest Essay, pp. 14-16.

VII. A Search for Solutions

1. Larry Marshall, "Synergistic Solutions: A Tapestry of Great Power," Speiser Contest Essay.
2. Jonathan Kwitny, *Endless Enemies: America's Worldwide War Against Its Own Best Interests* (New York: Congdon & Weed, 1984).
3. Peter Navarro, *The Policy Game: How Special Interests and Ideologues Are Stealing America* (New York: John Wiley & Sons, 1984).
4. Daniel Yergin and Martin Hillenbrand, eds., *Global Insecurity: A Strategy for Energy and Economic Renewal* (Boston: Houghton Mifflin, 1982).
5. Lester R. Brown et al., *State of the World, 1987* (New York: W.W. Norton, 1987); and Barry Commoner, *The Closing Circle—Nature, Man and Technology* (New York: Bantam, 1971).
6. Ilya Prigogine and Isabelle Stengers, *Order Out of Chaos: Man's New Dialogue with Nature* (New York: Bantam Books, 1984).
7. Marilyn Ferguson, *The Aquarian Conspiracy* (Los Angeles: J.P. Tarcher, 1980); and Fritjof Capra, *The Turning Point: Science, Society and the Rising Culture* (New York: Bantam Books, 1983)
8. Jonathan Schell, *The Fate of the Earth* (New York: Avon, 1982).
9. Freeman Dyson, *Weapons and Hope* (New York: Harper & Row, 1985); *Ground Zero: What About the Russians—And Nuclear War?* (New York: Pocketbooks, 1983); George F. Kennan, *The Nuclear Delusion* (New York: Pantheon Books, 1983); Amory B. and L. Hunter Lovins, *Brittle Power: Energy Strategy for National Security* (Andover, MA: Brick House, 1982); and Fred A. Wolf, *Star Wave: Mind, Consciousness and Quantum Physics* (New York: Macmillan, 1984), pp. 169-70.
10. Navarro, op. cit.
11. Ben Bova, *Star Peace: Assured Survival* (New York: Tom Doherty Associates, 1986); and General David Graham, *High Frontier: A Strategy for National Survival* (New York: Tom Doherty Associates, 1983).
12. Maxwell Maltz, *Psycho Cybernetics* (New York: Pocketbooks,

1983).
13. Roger Fisher and William Ury, *Getting to Yes: Negotiating Agreement Without Giving In* (New York: Penguin Books, 1983).
14. Zbigniew Brzezinski et al., eds., *Promise or Peril: The Strategic Defense Initiative* (Washington, DC: Ethics and Public Policy Center, 1986); and Union of Concerned Scientists Staff (John Tirman, ed.), *The Fallacy of Star Wars: Why Space Weapons Can't Protect Us* (New York: Vintage Books, Random House, 1984).
15. See, for example, Jonathan Schell, *The Abolition* (New York: Avon, 1986).
16. Bova and Graham, op. cit.
17. Larry Geis and Fabrice Florin, eds., *Moving Into Space: The Myths and Realities of Extraterrestrial Space* (New York: Perennial Library, 1978). See also T.A. Heppenheimer, *Colonies in Space* (New York: Warner Books, 1977); and Gerard K. O'Neill, *The High Frontier: Human Colonies in Space* (New York: Bantam Books, 1978).
18. A brief description and references for each of these plans can be found in Stuart M. Speiser, *The USOP Handbook* (New York: Council on International and Public Affairs, 1986), Chapter 10.
19. Emery Reves, *Anatomy of Peace* (New York: Harper & Brothers, 1944).
20. Gerald Mische, "SuperStock and World Order: A Natural Partnership," Speiser Contest Essay, pp. 11, 31-33.
21. Arnold Berger, "How to End the Nuclear Nightmare: Comments on the SuperStock Plan of Stuart M. Speiser," Speiser Contest Essay, pp. 12-13.
22. Thomas Moore, "Entering a New Age: How to Get There from Here," Speiser Contest Essay, pp. 8-9.
23. Christopher Budd, "The Metamorphasis of Capitalism," Speiser Contest Essay, p. 3.
24. Donald Clark, "Devolution: A Path to Stable Peace," Speiser Contest Essay, pp. 5-7.
25. Kevin Ketchum, "Expanding the Democratic Ideal: A Redefinition of Free Enterprise," Speiser Contest Essay, pp. 1-2.

Epilogue

1. *Time*, July 27, 1987.
2. Mikhail S. Gorbachev (Mimeo. release from the Soviet Mission, New York, 1987).

3.   Mikhail S. Gorbachev, *Perestroika* (New York: Harper & Row, 1987), pp. 211, 216-17.
4.   Ibid., pp. 83, 96-98.
5.   Stuart M. Speiser, *How to End the Nuclear Nightmare* (Croton-on-Hudson, NY: North River Press, 1984).
6.   Hugh Thomas, *Armed Truce: The Beginnings of the Cold War, 1945-1946* (New York: Atheneum, 1987). Excerpt from a *Time* magazine book review.
7.   Kenneth B. Taylor, "The Alpha Proposal," Speiser Contest Essay.

Appendix

1.   *National Data Book and Guide to Sources: Statistical Abstract of the U.S.,* 105th ed. (Washington, DC: US Interior Department, Bureau of the Census, 1985), p. xvii.
2.   Ibid., p. 378.
3.   Ibid.
4.   U.S. Department of Labor, Bureau of Labor Statistics, "The Employment Situation: August 1985" (September 1985), Table A-1, as cited in "Catholic Social Teaching and the U.S. Economy" (2nd draft) in *Origins,* 15, No. 7 (October 10, 1985), paragraph 137.
5.   Stuart M. Speiser, *How to End the Nuclear Nightmare* (Croton-on-Hudson: North River Press, 1984), pp. 138-40.
6.   Ibid., p. 129.
7.   Ibid., p. 138.
8.   *National Data Book,* op. cit., pp. 357, 359.
9.   Ibid.
10. *Time,* July 15, 1985, p. 47.

BIBLIOGRAPHY

Barraclough, Geoffrey. *An Introduction to Contemporary History.* Pelican Books, New York, 1967.

Bell, Daniel. *The Coming of Post-Industrial Society.* Basic Books, New York, 1973.

Blumberg, Barbara. *The New Deal and the Unemployed: The View from New York City.* Bucknell University Press, Lewisburg, 1977.

Boulding, Kenneth E. *The Image.* Vail-Ballou Press, Binghamton, NY, 1956.

Djilas, Milovan. *The New Class.* Frederick A. Praeger, New York, 1957.

Drinan, Robert. *Beyond the Nuclear Freeze.* Seabury Press, New York, 1983.

Easterlin, Richard. *Population, Labor Force and Long Swings in Economic Growth: The American Experience.* Columbia University Press, New York, 1968.

Eastman, Max. *Reflections on the Failure of Socialism.* Devin-Adair, New York, 1955.

Froman, Creel. *The Two American Political Systems: Society, Economics and Politics.* Prentice-Hall, Englewood Cliffs, NJ, 1984.

Fromm, Erich. *Marx's Concept of Man.* Frederick Ungar, New York, 1961.

Galbraith, John Kenneth. *American Capitalism.* Houghton Mifflin, Boston, 1956.

Green, Mark. *Winning Back America.* Bantam Books, New York, 1982.

Grenier, Paul. "The Common Task: Peace Through Convergence Toward Compatible Ideals." Speiser Contest Essay, 1986.

193

Ground Zero. What About the Russians and Nuclear War? Pocket Books, New York, 1983.

Harman, Willis W. *An Incomplete Guide to the Future.* W.W. Norton, New York, 1979.

Heilbroner, Robert L. *An Inquiry into the Human Prospect.* W.W. Norton, New York, 1980.

_____. *The Limits of American Capitalism.* Harper & Row, New York, 1966.

Howell, David. *The New Capitalism: Personal Ownership and Social Progress.* Center for Polity Studies, London, 1986.

John Paul II, Pope. *Laborem Excerens (On Human Work).* Daughters of St. Paul, Boston, 1981.

Jones, Thomas E. *Options for the Future.* Praeger Publishers, New York, 1980.

Kahn, Herman, William Brown and Leon Martel. *The Next 200 Years.* William Morrow, New York, 1976.

Kelso, Louis O. and Mortimer Adler. *The Capitalist Manifesto.* Greenwood Press, Westport, CT, 1958.

Kelso, Louis O. and Patricia Hetter. *Two-Factor Theory: The Economics of Reality.* Vintage Books, New York, 1967.

Kennan, George. *The Nuclear Delusion.* Pantheon Books, New York, 1976.

Krough, Kenneth K. "Making Universal Capitalism a Reality." Speiser Contest Essay, 1985.

Leontief, Wassily. *The Future of the World Economy.* Oxford University Press, Oxford, 1977.

Levitan, Sar A. *Programs in Aid of the Poor.* (5th ed.). John Hopkins University Press, Baltimore and London, 1985.

Marx, Karl. *Capital.* Sonnenschein, Lowery, London, 1887.

Masuda, Yoneji. *The Information Society.* World Future Society, Washington, DC, 1981.

McElvaine, Robert S. *The Great Depression: America 1929-41.* Times Books, New York, 1984.

Meadows, L., D.H. Meadows, J. Randers and W. Behrens III. *The Limits to Growth.* Signet Books, New York, 1972.

Mesarovic, Mihajlo and Edward Pestel. *Mankind at the Turning Point.* Signet Books, New York, 1976.

Murray, Charles. *Losing Ground.* Basic Books, New York, 1984.

Naisbitt, John. *Megatrends.* Warner Books, New York, 1982.

National Conference of Catholic Bishops. *Economic Justice for All: Catholic Social Teaching and the U.S. Economy.* National Conference, Washington, DC, 1986.

Neuberger, E. and W. Duffy. *Comparative Economic Systems: A Decision-Making Approach.* Allyn & Bacon, Boston, 1976.

Nixon, Russell A. "The Historical Development of the Conception and Implementation of Full Employment as Economic Policy" in *Solutions to Unemployment.* David C. Colander, ed. Harcourt, Brace Jovanovich, San Diego, 1981.

Overstreet, Harry. *The Mature Mind.* W. W. Norton, New York, 1949.

Popper, Karl L. *The Open Society and Its Enemies.* Princeton University Press, Princeton, NJ, 1950.

Rauch, Basil. *The History of the New Deal.* (2nd ed.). Octagon Books, New York, 1980.

Reich, Robert B. *The Next American Frontier.* Times Books, New York, 1980.

Samuelson, Paul A. *Economics,* (11th ed.). McGraw-Hill, New York, 1980.

Schlesinger, Arthur M., Jr. *The Age of Roosevelt: The Politics of Upheaval.* Houghton Mifflin, Boston, 1960.

Sedlak, John. "Modified SuperStock, Full Employment and Elimination of the Federal Debt." Speiser Contest Essay, 1985.

Servan-Schreiber, Jean-Jacques. *The World Challenge.* Simon & Schuster, New York, 1981.

Sivard, Ruth Leger. *World Military and Social Expenditures, 1983-85.* WMSE Publications, Leesburg, VA, 1985.

Speiser, Stuart M. *How to End the Nuclear Nightmare.* North River Press, Croton-on-Hudson, NY, 1984.

Taylor, Kenneth B. "The Alpha Proposal." Speiser Contest Essay, 1985.

Thurow, Lester C. "The Implications of Zero Economic Growth," *Challenge,* March/April 1977.

_____. *The Zero-Sum Society.* Basic Books, New York, 1980.

Tinberger, Jan, ed. *RIO: Reshaping the International Order.* E.P. Dutton, New York, 1977.

Toffler, Alvin. *The Third Wave.* William Morrow, New York, 1980.

Whyte, Lancelot. *The Next Development in Man.* New American Library, New York, 1950.

Wisman, Jon D. "Economic Reform for Humanity's Greatest Struggle." Speiser Contest Essay, 1986.